# dinner
# tonight

ALSO BY ALEX SNODGRASS
*The Comfortable Kitchen*
*The Defined Dish*

# dinner tonight

### 100 SIMPLE, HEALTHY RECIPES
### FOR EVERY NIGHT OF THE WEEK

## Alex Snodgrass

### PHOTOGRAPHY BY KRISTEN KILPATRICK

WILLIAM MORROW

*An Imprint of HarperCollinsPublishers*

**To Clayton,
Sutton, and Winnie,**
*dinner time with you is my favorite.*

# contents

1 INTRODUCTION

5 CONVENIENT CONDIMENTS

13 SALADS

45 SOUPS

71 PASTA AND NOODLES

97 POULTRY

133 BEEF, PORK, AND LAMB

169 SEAFOOD

197 VEGETARIAN

215 DESSERTS

233 ACKNOWLEDGMENTS

237 UNIVERSAL CONVERSION CHART

239 INDEX

# introduction

Since writing my first cookbook years ago, my goal has always been to share my love of cooking through simple, wholesome recipes that give you a taste of the joy that cooking brings me. And while home-cooked meals and time around the table sharing with those you love is something ingrained in me from my own childhood, as a mother of two, I know it is not always possible to execute. Yes, even I turn to takeout from time to time!

While we all strive to have a home-cooked meal on the table for everyone to enjoy together each night, I fully understand how the stress of life can make that a distant reality and dampen the joy cooking should bring to us all. Between getting the kids to their activities, working late hours, keeping up with social events, and, well, just being tired, the fun of cooking can quickly disappear.

But delicious and nutritious food doesn't always have to be complicated. Over the years, I've found various tips and tricks to make meals easier, and for my third book, I want to provide simplified, delicious recipes that our busy lives demand so that you can get dinner on the table tonight with less stress.

Even if you are like me and adore the process of cooking, I can still relate to not looking forward to all the cleanup a home-cooked meal requires. That's why you'll see a bountiful collection of skillet dinners, one-pot meals, and sheet pan dinners here, to make your kitchen cleanup a little less daunting. To some people taking shortcuts, like cooking in one pot, can mean less flavor, but rest assured that the recipes in this book are some of my absolute favorites, streamlined to be as straightforward as possible by using a minimal number of pots and pans but never sacrificing taste.

And to create lots of flavor in a shorter amount of time—since having busy lives means needing to make easy and satisfying meals with a little less planning and prep—you'll find yourself turning to your pantry for convenient sauces for flavorful last-minute meals. When you have flavor-packed store-bought ingredients on hand, like a bottle of BBQ sauce, a jar of gochujang, or pesto, there's an extra helping hand in the kitchen to get dinner on the table with a little less stress and fewer groceries to pick up that day.

The chapters within *Dinner Tonight* are filled with recipes that are here to make life a little easier. Approachable dinners like my Simple Skillet Beef Shawarma (page 144), Saucy Gochujang Chicken Stir-Fry (page 108), or my Green Chile Chicken and Rice Soup (page 57) will bring fast flavor even if you've just walked in the door from work. There are also some delicious build-your-own bowl recipes that are meant to bring your loved ones around the table and have some fun. Recipes like Baked Salmon Sushi Bowls with Spicy Mayo (page 173), Slow Cooker or Pressure Cooker Gochujang Shredded Beef Bowls (page 139), and Red Pepper Miso Buddha Bowls (page 208) encourage everyone to choose their own journey and build their plates according to their preferences, which I find is a wonderful way to get picky eaters to try new things.

You'll also find some comforting classics, like Sour Cream Chicken Enchiladas (page 107), Sheet Pan Mini BBQ-Cheddar Meatloaves with Sweet Potatoes and Brussels Sprouts (page 159), and Skillet Chicken Cacciatore (page 101), that take me back to my family table growing up while still using simple and straightforward techniques. Who says you can't have home cooking in a hurry?

As you flip through and cook the recipes within this book, I hope you'll find yourself inspired and encouraged that you, too, can create delicious meals any night of the week. I hope my recipes empower you to cook more often and allow you to spend more time enjoying the meals you create with friends, family, or just yourself.

Whether it be for dinner with your family on a Tuesday or a party with your friends, this is your friendly reminder to always keep cooking fun, welcoming, and an expression of your love for the people around your table.

# convenient condiments

**D**inner Tonight is all about reminding you that cooking at home doesn't have to be a hassle. Having store-bought sauces and other condiments on hand makes it easy to throw together a satisfying meal quickly. While making things from scratch can be more delicious, it can also be time-consuming, and sometimes we just need dinner on the table a little more quickly with a little less effort.

To help stock your kitchen, here's what I think are the best condiments to have on hand for quick and easy meals. And while these are mostly my store-bought favorites, I have included a few recipes for when you do have the time for a homemade condiment.

### BARBECUE SAUCE

Put that bottle of BBQ sauce in your pantry to work! This is one of those condiments that lends itself to adding such a big flavor with even a small amount. It can enhance your everyday weeknight dinner with that perfect saucy, slightly spicy—depending on your BBQ sauce—and a little bit sweet hit to dinners like my Skillet BBQ Chicken Quinoa Bake (page 111) and Sheet Pan Mini BBQ-Cheddar Meatloaves with Sweet Potatoes and Brussels Sprouts (page 159). Both are top favorites in my family.

### BUFFALO SAUCE

Buffalo sauce makes my heart flutter. It's got the spice and the tang, and it adds a rich flavor to dishes. I love to use it on salads and sandwiches, but my favorite way? In the Crispy Buffalo Chicken Lettuce Wraps with Blue Cheese Sauce (page 102).

### DIJON MUSTARD

Dijon mustard makes my cooking world go round. It works as an emulsifier in salad dressings and pan sauces, and its flavor pairs well with everything from chicken to steak, which means it's a staple that I reach for anytime I want to make that weeknight dinner. You'll find it throughout the book, but I especially love it in recipes like Sheet Pan Hot Honey Dijon Chicken (page 115) and Philly Cheesesteak–Stuffed Mushrooms (page 153).

### GOCHUJANG

This fermented Korean chile paste adds instant flavor in recipes throughout this book. If you've never had gochujang before, try it in marinades for meat dishes, stirred into dipping sauces, or used to punch up stews or soups. A tub of gochujang lasts a while because a little bit goes a long way, but I promise you'll be putting it to good use in Slow Cooker or Pressure Cooker Gochujang Shredded Beef Bowls (page 139), 2 a.m. Kimchi Noodles (page 76), and Saucy Gochujang Chicken Stir-Fry (page 108). Note, however, that gochujang is often made with a small bit of wheat to help the paste firm up, making it a little difficult to find a gluten-free option, but the Coconut Secret brand, which is made with coconut aminos, can be found online and at various grocers.

### GREEK YOGURT

I like to use Greek yogurt as a substitute for sour cream or heavy cream in recipes. It's a little bit lower in fat, it's higher in protein, and it adds tang and creaminess to recipes like Deconstructed Waldorf Salad (page 43), Jerk-Inspired Chicken Tacos (page 125), and Herby Mediterranean Baked Meatballs (page 147).

### HARISSA

Harissa is a North African paste made of roasted chiles and spices. It has a smoky and spicy flavor, although the level of heat varies from brand to brand. It can be used to add immediate flavor to soups, salads, and skillet dinners. I use it quite a bit throughout this book in recipes like my Herby Harissa Lamb Pasta (page 79) and Harissa Fish en Papillote (page 178). I recommend the Mina brand harissa sauce, but definitely go with the mild version if your palate is more sensitive.

# homemade mayo

**MAKES 1 CUP**

GLUTEN-FREE
DAIRY-FREE
PALEO
WHOLE30
GRAIN-FREE
VEGETARIAN

1 cup avocado oil or other light-flavored oil

1 large egg

**OPTIONAL**

1 garlic clove, minced

1 teaspoon freshly squeezed lemon juice

2 teaspoons mustard powder

Kosher salt, to taste

*This recipe has been in all my books because it is incredibly easy to make and is the best base for creamy salad dressings and sauces—it's something that I use weekly in my kitchen. If you opt for store-bought, I suggest finding one that's made with avocado oil and is neutral in flavor. I personally prefer Sir Kensington brand!*

*Use the simple oil and egg emulsion below if I call for homemade mayo in the recipes in this book, or turn it into a more traditional mayonnaise by blending in the optional ingredients. It will keep for 5 to 7 days in the fridge.*

POUR the oil into a wide-mouth glass jar with an opening a little bit wider than the head of your immersion blender. Crack the egg into the oil and let it settle on the bottom of the jar.

PLACE the immersion blender in the jar and position the blade directly over the egg yolk. Turn the immersion blender on low and hold in place, with the blender running, until the ingredients at the bottom of the jar start to turn into a creamy emulsion, about 10 seconds.

START lifting the blender up a bit and pressing it back down, bringing the mixture above the mayo at the bottom into the emulsion, bit by bit, until you reach the top and the entire jar is emulsified. Blend in any optional ingredients, if desired.

# lemon basil pesto

**MAKES 1 CUP**

½ cup extra-virgin olive oil

2 tablespoons freshly squeezed lemon juice (about 1 lemon)

3 garlic cloves, peeled

½ cup salted roasted cashews

¼ cup pine nuts

2 cups packed fresh basil leaves

Kosher salt

Freshly ground black pepper

*While there is really nothing quite as wonderful as homemade pesto, I almost always have a jar of store-bought pesto on hand. It's a great way to amp up a sandwich or use in a last-minute pantry pasta, but you'll see that I use pesto in a variety of ways in this book, including in my Sheet Pan Sausage and Sweet Piquanté Peppers (page 143), One-Skillet Lasagna (page 80), and Sun-Dried Tomato, Pesto, and Mint Pasta (page 87).*

*Also, when I have fresh basil that is starting to fade, I often whip it up into this simple pesto and freeze it in an ice cube tray. That way I can pull the prepared cubes out of the freezer to easily add flavor to meals. Here is my go-to homemade recipe if time permits!*

IN a food processor or blender, combine the oil, lemon juice, garlic, cashews, pine nuts, and basil and blend until smooth. Add salt and pepper to taste.

### MILD DICED GREEN CHILES

If you've been cooking my recipes for a while, you already know these chiles are commonly found in my recipes! They add the perfect amount of flavor and with the mild version, not too much heat—even for sensitive palates. They add delicious flavor to recipes like my Chipotle Turkey–Stuffed Poblano Peppers (page 112) and Crunchy Baked Beef Tacos (page 156).

### MISO

Miso is a secret weapon in the kitchen to add immediate and bold flavor to any soup, salad dressing, or roasted vegetable. Miso, a Japanese fermented paste, is made from various beans and/or grains. The beans used can include soybeans, chickpeas, and adzuki beans, all of which are gluten-free. Grains used can include gluten-free examples, such as rice, millet, amaranth, or quinoa; or miso can be made with wheat, barley, or rye, which are not gluten-free. To keep my miso dishes gluten-free, you'll need to look closely for a brand of miso paste that is gluten-free. I like Miso Master's Organic Mellow White Miso, which is marked as certified gluten-free. Try it in my Red Pepper Miso Buddha Bowls (page 208).

### PICKLED JALAPEÑOS

I love using pickled jalapeños to add quick flavor to sauces as they have a more subtle jalapeño flavor, are less spicy than fresh jalapeños, and have a strong vinegar flavor. You must try the Blackened Sheet Pan Salmon with Jalapeño Tartar Sauce (page 190); the sauce will be your new favorite!

### SALSA VERDE

Oh, the things I can do with a jar of salsa verde—also known as tomatillo salsa—in my kitchen. One of my favorite convenient condiments, it easily goes on any taco, but it can also be used to amp up soups and other weeknight dinners, like my Sour Cream Chicken Enchiladas (page 107) and Chipotle Cauliflower Tostadas (page 198).

### SRIRACHA

Sriracha is a bright-red, extremely versatile hot sauce that is most commonly associated with Vietnamese and Thai cuisine, although it's become one of the most popular condiments in American grocery stores. It is made from red chile peppers, garlic, vinegar, salt, and, typically, sugar, and can be used to add spice and flavor to

anything from noodle soup to chicken wings. I use it throughout this book in recipes like Baked Salmon Sushi Bowls with Spicy Mayo (page 173), Aromatic Shrimp and Noodle Soup (page 58), and Bang Bang Shrimp Lettuce Wraps (page 193). Be sure to check your labels to find Whole30-compatible sriracha; my favorite is the Yellowbird brand.

## SUN-DRIED TOMATOES

Sun-dried tomatoes packed in olive oil can be used in salads, pastas, and countless other dishes when you desire a punch of intense tomato flavor. They're found in one of my favorite recipes in the book, Sun-Dried Tomato, Pesto, and Mint Pasta (page 87).

## THAI CURRY PASTE

Curry paste adds big, bright, powerful flavors to dishes, and it's one of the easiest ways to bring a simple dinner to life. You'll see that I typically tend to gravitate toward green and red curry pastes. Traditional Thai red curry paste can feature up to twenty different dried chiles, among them bird's eye chiles and Thai long chiles. Thai green curry paste features many of the same chiles as red but in their fresh green state as opposed to dried, plus cilantro and makrut lime leaves to give it a vibrant, green color. You can try recipes using these, such as my One-Pot Green Curry Veggie Noodles (page 84) and Skillet Chicken and Veggies with "Peanut" Sauce (page 122). I recommend the Mae Ploy brand.

14  SHREDDED KALE SALAD WITH GRAPEFRUIT
    AND SEARED SALMON

17  CALIFORNIA TURKEY SALAD WITH RASPBERRY
    VINAIGRETTE

18  SEARED TUNA WITH WHITE BEAN AND ARUGULA SALAD

21  CURRIED CHICKEN AND KALE SALAD WITH
    CREAMY HARISSA DRESSING

22  GRILLED CHICKEN SALAD WITH CHILI-LIME DRESSING

24  SHEET PAN SALMON NIÇOISE

27  THAI-INSPIRED STEAK SALAD

28  FATTOUSH SALAD WITH CREAMY FETA DRESSING

31  BLT PANZANELLA

32  WARM FARRO STEAK SALAD

35  CREAMY ITALIAN CHOPPED SALAD

36  CAJUN COBB SALAD WITH SHRIMP

39  MACHO SALAD

40  SWEET POTATO FRY SALAD WITH LEMON-TAHINI
    DRESSING

43  DECONSTRUCTED WALDORF SALAD

salads

# shredded kale salad with grapefruit and seared salmon

**MAKES 4 SERVINGS** • **TOTAL TIME: 35 MINUTES**

### FOR THE APPLE CIDER VINAIGRETTE

2 tablespoons extra-virgin olive oil

2 tablespoons apple cider vinegar

1 teaspoon Dijon mustard

1 teaspoon honey

¼ teaspoon smoked paprika

½ teaspoon kosher salt

½ teaspoon freshly ground black pepper

### FOR THE SALMON

4 skin-on center-cut salmon fillets (6 ounces each), pin bones removed

1 teaspoon kosher salt

½ teaspoon freshly ground black pepper

1 tablespoon extra-virgin olive oil

1 tablespoon freshly squeezed lemon juice (about ½ lemon)

### FOR THE SALAD

2 bunches lacinato kale, deribbed and thinly sliced (about 8 cups)

1 Honeycrisp apple, halved and thinly sliced

½ cup salted dry-roasted almonds, roughly chopped

1 medium grapefruit, cut into supremes (see note)

½ cup grated aged cheddar cheese (omit for dairy-free and paleo)

*I know kale salads have a bad reputation for being, well . . . dull! Inspired by one of my favorite fast-casual restaurants, Flower Child, this simple kale salad is far from dull. It's easy to make but the flavors are bright, tangy, and beautiful. While I serve mine with salmon, any protein works great with this salad! Rotisserie chicken, sautéed shrimp, or even a seared steak work well here. You can really have fun with it, and this will quickly become your go-to kale salad.*

**MAKE THE APPLE CIDER VINAIGRETTE:** In a small bowl, whisk together the dressing ingredients until well combined. Set aside.

**PREPARE THE SALMON:** Season the salmon fillets with the salt and pepper. In a large nonstick skillet, heat the oil over medium-high heat. When hot, add the salmon skin side down and cook it on one side until golden and crisp, about 4 minutes. Carefully flip the fillets and reduce the heat to medium. Continue to cook until the salmon is done to your liking and flakes easily with a fork, 4 to 5 more minutes. Transfer the cooked salmon to a plate and finish with the lemon juice. Tent with foil to keep warm.

**ASSEMBLE THE SALAD:** In a large bowl, combine the kale, apple, and almonds. Pour the dressing over the salad and toss continuously until the kale is well coated and has slightly wilted, 3 to 4 minutes.

**ADD** the grapefruit and the grated cheddar (if using) and gently toss once more. Divide among four bowls and top with the salmon.

## FROM MY KITCHEN TO YOURS

To make beautiful, juicy little grapefruit segments with no pith or skin, set the peeled grapefruit on a cutting board and use a thin, sharp paring knife to cut down the sides of the fruit, just through the remaining pith and membranes, to reveal the flesh underneath. Then use the knife to remove each segment of grapefruit by cutting along the sides of the segments to release them from the membranes, removing the seeds as you go.

# california turkey salad with raspberry vinaigrette

**MAKES 4 SERVINGS** • **TOTAL TIME: 25 MINUTES**

GLUTEN-FREE

GRAIN-FREE

*if modified:*

DAIRY-FREE

PALEO

WHOLE30

## FOR THE RASPBERRY VINAIGRETTE

1 cup raspberries

¼ cup extra-virgin olive oil

2 teaspoons Dijon mustard

1 tablespoon freshly squeezed lemon juice (about ½ lemon)

1 tablespoon champagne vinegar

2 teaspoons honey (omit for Whole30)

1 garlic clove, peeled

½ teaspoon chipotle chile powder

1 teaspoon kosher salt

½ teaspoon freshly ground black pepper

## FOR THE SALAD

8 cups baby arugula

2 cups alfalfa or broccoli sprouts

½ cup halved and thinly sliced red onion (about ½ small onion)

1 large avocado, thinly sliced

1 pound very thinly sliced no-sugar-added smoked turkey

1 cup freshly grated Havarti cheese (omit for dairy-free, paleo, and Whole30)

½ cup slivered almonds, toasted (see note)

*When you are short on time, this salad is the perfect recipe to make for a simple meal. The raspberry vinaigrette comes together in minutes to create a naturally sweet and savory dressing that adds the perfect pop of flavor to any simple salad. Here, I serve the dressing over a California-inspired salad filled with creamy avocado, buttery Havarti cheese, peppery arugula, toasted almonds, crunchy sprouts, and deli turkey.*

**MAKE THE RASPBERRY VINAIGRETTE:** In a blender or using an immersion blender in a wide-mouth jar, combine the raspberries, oil, mustard, lemon juice, vinegar, honey (if using), garlic, chile powder, salt, and pepper. Begin blending on medium-low, then slowly increase the speed until the dressing is smooth and fully combined. This keeps in the fridge for 3 to 5 days.

**ASSEMBLE THE SALAD:** In a large bowl, combine the arugula and sprouts and toss. Divide the arugula and sprouts onto four plates and top with the red onion. Add one-quarter of the avocado to each plate, fanning the slices out on one corner of the plate. Tear the turkey into bite-size pieces and place it in the corner of each plate opposite the avocado. Sprinkle each plate with the cheese (if using) and slivered almonds. Drizzle each with the desired amount of dressing.

## FROM MY KITCHEN TO YOURS

Toasting your almonds draws out the natural oils to enhance their flavor and add some extra crunch! To do this, simply add the slivered almonds to a dry (no oil) medium skillet over medium heat. Warm the almonds, tossing occasionally, until you begin to smell the toasted almonds and they are golden brown. Remove the pan from the heat and transfer the almonds to a plate to let them cool.

# seared tuna with white bean and arugula salad

**MAKES 2 SERVINGS** • **TOTAL TIME: 25 MINUTES**

### FOR THE WHITE BEAN SALAD

3 tablespoons extra-virgin olive oil

½ teaspoon Dijon mustard

Grated zest of ½ lemon

1 tablespoon freshly squeezed lemon juice (about ½ lemon)

1 tablespoon red wine vinegar

¼ teaspoon crushed red pepper flakes

½ teaspoon kosher salt

½ teaspoon freshly ground black pepper

One 15-ounce can cannellini beans, drained and rinsed

¼ cup halved lengthwise and thinly sliced shallot (about ½ large shallot)

1 tablespoon roughly chopped drained capers

½ cup roughly chopped fresh parsley leaves

1 tablespoon finely chopped fresh oregano or ½ teaspoon dried

### FOR THE TUNA

Two 1½-inch-thick bigeye or ahi tuna fillets (about 6 ounces each)

½ teaspoon kosher salt

½ teaspoon freshly ground black pepper

2 tablespoons extra-virgin olive oil

### FOR ASSEMBLY

4 cups baby arugula

½ lemon, cut into wedges, for serving

*This quick salad is bursting with Mediterranean flavors. I love the creaminess of the white beans paired with the peppery arugula and a simple and herby vinaigrette. Topped with quick-seared tuna, this dish feels elegant enough to serve for a special occasion but comes together quickly enough for a weeknight meal. In a bind, feel free to use canned tuna that is packed in olive oil and skip the cooking altogether.*

**MAKE THE WHITE BEAN SALAD:** In a medium bowl, whisk together the oil, mustard, lemon zest, lemon juice, vinegar, pepper flakes, salt, and black pepper until well combined and emulsified. Add the beans, shallot, capers, parsley, and oregano and gently toss to combine. Transfer to the fridge until ready to serve.

**COOK THE TUNA:** Season the tuna evenly on both sides with the salt and pepper. In a large nonstick skillet, heat the oil over medium-high heat. When the oil is hot and shimmering, place the tuna in the skillet and sear it for 1 to 2 minutes per side, until a golden-brown crust has formed but the inside is still rare. Transfer the tuna to a cutting board and use a sharp knife to cut it into thin slices.

**ASSEMBLE THE SALAD:** Immediately before serving, toss the arugula in with the white bean mixture until just combined. Divide the white bean and arugula salad between two plates. Top with the sliced tuna and serve with lemon wedges.

# curried chicken and kale salad with creamy harissa dressing

**MAKES 4 SERVINGS • TOTAL TIME: 30 MINUTES**

## FOR THE CREAMY HARISSA DRESSING

¼ cup crumbled goat cheese

2 tablespoons extra-virgin olive oil

2 tablespoons spicy or mild harissa sauce (I use Mina brand)

2 tablespoons freshly squeezed lemon juice (about 1 lemon)

1 teaspoon champagne vinegar

2 teaspoons honey

¼ teaspoon kosher salt

½ teaspoon freshly ground black pepper

## FOR THE CHICKEN

1½ pounds boneless, skinless chicken breast, cut into ½-inch cubes

2 tablespoons extra-virgin olive oil

1 teaspoon kosher salt

½ teaspoon freshly ground black pepper

1 teaspoon curry powder

1 teaspoon garlic powder

½ teaspoon smoked paprika

½ teaspoon ground cumin

1 tablespoon freshly squeezed lemon juice (about ½ lemon)

## FOR THE SALAD

8 cups deribbed and finely chopped lacinato kale (about 2 bunches)

2 cups baby arugula

1 medium Honeycrisp apple, cored and cut into 2-inch-long thin matchsticks

¼ cup golden raisins

½ cup salted roasted pumpkin seeds

¼ cup roughly chopped fresh dill

## FOR SERVING

⅓ cup crumbled goat cheese

¼ cup roughly chopped fresh dill

*This delicious and nutritious kale salad is filled with so many delightful flavors! The creamy dressing comes together quickly by simply blending goat cheese with a store-bought harissa and a few additional ingredients. The result is out-of-this-world flavor. The dressing is then tossed with kale, apples, golden raisins, and crunchy pumpkin seeds and topped off with warm chicken that is sautéed with curry powder and cumin. All the flavors marry together so beautifully for the perfect salad! This is a great meal prep–friendly lunch—simply store the components in separate containers until you're ready to serve.*

**MAKE THE CREAMY HARISSA DRESSING:** In a blender or using an immersion blender in a wide-mouth jar, combine the dressing ingredients. Blend until the dressing is completely smooth. Set aside while you assemble the rest of the salad. This keeps in the fridge for 3 to 5 days.

**COOK THE CHICKEN:** Pat the chicken dry with paper towels. In a large skillet, heat the oil over medium heat. Add the chicken to the skillet and season with the salt, pepper, curry powder, garlic powder, smoked paprika, and cumin. Toss to combine and cook, tossing occasionally, until the chicken is cooked through and golden brown on all sides, 6 to 8 minutes. During the last minute of cooking, add the lemon juice to deglaze the pan. Toss to combine until each piece is evenly coated with lemon and spices. Remove from the heat and set aside.

**ASSEMBLE THE SALAD:** In a large bowl, combine the kale, arugula, apple, raisins, pumpkin seeds, and dill. Pour a few tablespoons of the dressing onto the salad and toss until the kale is evenly coated and slightly wilted, 1 to 2 minutes.

**DIVIDE** the salad among four bowls, then evenly distribute the warm cooked chicken over it. Finish with the goat cheese crumbles, a drizzle of extra dressing, and the dill.

# grilled chicken salad with chili-lime dressing

**MAKES 4 SERVINGS** • **TOTAL TIME: 40 MINUTES**

## FOR THE CHILI-LIME DRESSING

½ cup extra-virgin olive oil

3 garlic cloves, minced

1 teaspoon anchovy paste or 2 oil-packed anchovy fillets

¼ cup freshly squeezed lime juice (about 2 limes)

1 teaspoon chili powder

½ teaspoon paprika

½ teaspoon crushed red pepper flakes

½ teaspoon dried oregano

½ teaspoon kosher salt

¼ teaspoon cayenne pepper

## FOR THE CHICKEN AND BACON

1½ pounds boneless, skinless chicken breasts

1 teaspoon kosher salt

½ teaspoon freshly ground black pepper

½ teaspoon ground cumin

½ teaspoon paprika

4 slices no-sugar-added bacon, roughly chopped

## FOR THE SALAD

8 cups chopped romaine lettuce (about 2 large heads)

1 cup halved cherry tomatoes

¼ cup halved and thinly sliced red onion (about ¼ small onion)

¾ cup freshly shredded sharp cheddar cheese (omit for dairy-free, paleo, and Whole30)

1 avocado, sliced

1 cup crushed white corn tortilla chips (omit for paleo, Whole30, and grain-free)

*If you are from the DFW Metroplex, you most likely recognize where the inspiration for this salad came from, and if you're not familiar, Mi Cocina is a very popular Tex-Mex restaurant I grew up eating at. The Rico Salad is a go-to order of mine, so I've made my own rendition, and I am quite obsessed with it. The chili-lime dressing is exquisite alone, but pairing it with lettuce, bacon, tomato, and crispy tortilla chips creates a salad that will quickly become one of your all-time favorites, too.*

**MAKE THE CHILI-LIME DRESSING:** In a blender or using an immersion blender in a wide-mouth jar, combine all the dressing ingredients and blend until smooth. Set aside. This keeps in the fridge for 5 to 7 days.

**COOK THE CHICKEN AND BACON:** Place the chicken breasts on a cutting board and cover with parchment paper or plastic wrap. Using a meat mallet or the bottom of a heavy skillet, pound the chicken to a uniform ½-inch thickness. Pat dry with paper towels. Season the chicken on both sides evenly with the salt, pepper, cumin, and paprika. Set aside.

**LINE** a plate with paper towels. Add the chopped bacon to a cold large skillet. Turn the heat to medium and cook until the bacon is crisp, 7 to 9 minutes total, stirring occasionally. Using a slotted spoon, transfer the bacon to the plate lined with paper towels and set aside. Reserve the bacon fat in the skillet.

**INCREASE** the heat under the skillet with the bacon fat to medium-high. Add the chicken to the pan and cook until golden brown and cooked through, 4 to 5 minutes per side. Transfer the chicken to a clean cutting board and let it rest.

**ASSEMBLE THE SALAD:** In a large bowl, combine the romaine, tomatoes, onion, and cheese (if using). Drizzle with the desired amount of dressing and toss to coat. Divide the salad among four plates, placing it in the center. Surround the salad with avocado slices.

**CUT** the chicken into ½-inch-thick strips. Place the sliced chicken around each of the salads, alternating with the avocado slices, and sprinkle with the bacon and the crumbled tortilla chips (if using).

# sheet pan salmon niçoise

**MAKES 4 SERVINGS** • **TOTAL TIME: 50 MINUTES**

## FOR THE POTATOES

1 pound baby Dutch yellow potatoes, halved

1 tablespoon extra-virgin olive oil

½ teaspoon dried oregano

½ teaspoon dried thyme

½ teaspoon kosher salt

¼ teaspoon freshly ground black pepper

## FOR THE VINAIGRETTE

½ teaspoon anchovy paste

1 teaspoon Dijon mustard

⅓ cup extra-virgin olive oil

3 tablespoons freshly squeezed lemon juice (about 1½ lemons)

1 garlic clove, minced

¼ teaspoon dried thyme

½ teaspoon dried oregano

Kosher salt and freshly ground black pepper, to taste

## FOR THE SHEET PAN

1 pound salmon fillet, skinned, pin bones removed

½ pound haricots verts (French green beans)

1½ tablespoons extra-virgin olive oil, divided

¾ teaspoon kosher salt, divided

½ teaspoon dried oregano

½ teaspoon dried thyme

½ teaspoon freshly ground black pepper, divided

*Niçoise salad is one of my absolute favorite things on the planet, with so many delicious ingredients packed into one big, filling salad with lots of umami flavors. Although easy to make, it does have a lot of moving parts. Here, in this salmon version, I've taken a few of the steps out by placing the potatoes, salmon, and green beans on a sheet pan to roast in the oven while you make the dressing and assemble the rest of the salad for a seamless, simplified Niçoise.*

**PREHEAT** the oven to 375°F. Line a large sheet pan with parchment paper.

**PARBAKE THE POTATOES:** Spread the potatoes onto the prepared sheet pan in a single layer. Add the oil, oregano, thyme, salt, and pepper. Toss until the potatoes are coated. Parbake the potatoes for 20 minutes (this is done before you add the salmon and additional veggies, as the potatoes need more time to cook).

**MEANWHILE, MAKE THE VINAIGRETTE:** Combine all the vinaigrette ingredients in a small jar or bowl. Shake or whisk until well combined. Set aside.

**CONTINUE WITH THE SHEET PAN:** After the potatoes have been in for 20 minutes, remove the pan from the oven. Toss the potatoes and move them to one side of the sheet pan. Place the salmon in the center and the haricots verts on the other side. Drizzle 1 tablespoon of the oil on the salmon and rub it into the flesh until it is evenly coated. Season the salmon with ½ teaspoon of the salt, the oregano, thyme, and ¼ teaspoon of the pepper.

**DRIZZLE** the remaining ½ tablespoon oil over the haricots verts and season with the remaining ¼ teaspoon salt and the remaining ¼ teaspoon pepper and toss to coat.

**RETURN** the sheet pan to the oven and roast until the salmon is cooked through and easily flakes with a fork, 18 to 20 minutes.

**MEANWHILE, FOR THE SALAD:** Make the jammy eggs. Set up a bowl of ice and water. Bring a small saucepan of water to a boil. Using a slotted spoon, carefully lower the eggs into the boiling water; cook for 7½ minutes, then use a slotted spoon to transfer them to the ice water. This will result in eggs with the whites set and the yolks jammy. Set aside.

**FOR THE SALAD**

4 large eggs

4 cups roughly chopped butter lettuce (about 1 large head)

1 cup halved cherry tomatoes

½ cup pitted Niçoise olives, torn (sub kalamata olives)

2 tablespoons capers, drained and rinsed

½ cup halved and thinly sliced red onion (about ½ small onion)

**TO SERVE:** Divide the lettuce, cherry tomatoes, olives, capers, and red onion among four plates. Using a fork, flake the salmon and divide the flaked salmon pieces among the plates, along with the potatoes and haricots verts. Peel and halve each of the eggs and place on each plate. Drizzle with the desired amount of vinaigrette.

# thai-inspired steak salad

**MAKES 4 SERVINGS** • **TOTAL TIME: 35 MINUTES**

### FOR THE DRESSING

¼ cup extra-virgin olive oil

¼ cup freshly squeezed lime juice (about 2 limes)

2 tablespoons fish sauce (I use Red Boat brand)

1 tablespoon coconut aminos

1 tablespoon coconut sugar

2 garlic cloves, minced

1 to 3 fresh Thai chiles (1 for mild, 3 for hot), thinly sliced

### FOR THE SALAD

4 cups thinly sliced Savoy or napa cabbage (about ½ head)

2 cups halved and thinly sliced (on the diagonal) English cucumber (about 1 cucumber)

1 cup halved grape tomatoes

1 cup halved and thinly sliced red onion (about ½ onion)

½ cup roughly torn fresh mint leaves, plus more for garnish

½ cup fresh cilantro leaves, plus more for garnish

½ cup roughly chopped unsalted dry-roasted peanuts, plus more for garnish

½ teaspoon kosher salt

4 cups baby spring mix

### FOR THE STEAKS

4 filet mignon steaks (6 to 8 ounces each)

1 teaspoon kosher salt

½ teaspoon freshly ground black pepper

2 tablespoons extra-virgin olive oil

2 teaspoons toasted sesame oil

*If you are looking for something healthy that will also satisfy your taste buds, look no further than this Thai-inspired steak salad. Loaded with veggies, a tangy dressing, and delicious seared steak, this salad is packed with familiar Thai flavors, but so easy to prepare! I add Savoy cabbage to the base of this salad for extra crunch and to make this salad sturdy. That way, it keeps longer if you're making it ahead of time and stands up to the weight of the steak.*

**MAKE THE DRESSING:** In a small bowl, combine the dressing ingredients and whisk until the sugar is dissolved. Set aside. This keeps in the fridge for 5 to 7 days.

**MAKE THE SALAD:** In a large bowl, combine the cabbage, cucumber, tomatoes, onion, mint, cilantro, peanuts, and salt. Do not add the spring mix yet. Set aside while you cook the steak.

**COOK THE STEAKS:** Pat the steaks very dry with a paper towel. Season them on both sides with the salt and pepper, pressing the seasoning into the meat. In a large skillet, preferably cast-iron, heat the olive oil and sesame oil over medium-high heat. When the oil is shimmering, add the steaks and cook until a deep brown crust has formed and they are cooked to your preferred doneness, 3 to 4 minutes per side for medium-rare, 5 to 6 minutes per side for more well-done. Transfer the steaks to a cutting board and let rest for 8 to 10 minutes. Slice the steaks into thin pieces.

**IMMEDIATELY** before serving, pour ⅓ cup of the dressing over the salad and toss until well coated. Add the baby spring mix to the salad and gently toss again to combine. Divide the salad among four plates and top each salad with sliced steak. Drizzle the steak with the remaining dressing. Garnish with some chopped peanuts, mint leaves, and cilantro.

VEGETARIAN

*if modified:*

GLUTEN-FREE

# fattoush salad with creamy feta dressing

**MAKES 4 SERVINGS** • **TOTAL TIME: 30 MINUTES**

## FOR THE TOASTED PITA

2 pitas, roughly torn into 1-inch pieces
(sub gluten-free pita)

2 tablespoons extra-virgin olive oil

½ teaspoon Aleppo pepper

¼ teaspoon kosher salt

## FOR THE FETA DRESSING

4 ounces feta cheese (block, not
precrumbled)

¼ cup extra-virgin olive oil

2 tablespoons red wine vinegar

2 tablespoons freshly squeezed lemon
juice (about 1 lemon)

2 garlic cloves, roughly chopped

1 teaspoon Dijon mustard

1 teaspoon honey

½ teaspoon dried oregano

¼ teaspoon kosher salt

¼ teaspoon freshly ground black
pepper

## FOR THE SALAD

8 cups torn Little Gem lettuce or
roughly chopped romaine lettuce

2 cups medium-diced Persian (mini)
cucumbers (about 4 cucumbers)

2 cups medium-diced Roma (plum)
tomatoes (about 3 tomatoes)

1 cup small-diced red onion
(about 1 small onion)

½ cup finely chopped fresh dill

½ cup finely chopped fresh mint leaves

¼ cup finely chopped fresh parsley
leaves

2 ounces feta cheese, roughly
crumbled into small pieces, for serving

*This salad is my take on fattoush, a classic salad you'll find at all Lebanese restaurants and throughout the Middle East. It's a fresh and bright salad made with seasonal vegetables and topped with the all-important crisped pita bread. Not an authentic fattoush, my version includes a simple, delectable creamy feta dressing. The salad is great as is, but if you're wanting to bump it up with some protein, you should absolutely add the Simple Skillet Beef Shawarma (page 144).*

PREHEAT the oven to 375°F.

TOAST THE PITAS: Lay the pita pieces on a large sheet pan. Drizzle with the oil and sprinkle evenly with the Aleppo and salt. Gently toss to coat and spread across the sheet pan in a single layer. Bake until the pita is just crisp, about 8 minutes.

MEANWHILE, MAKE THE FETA DRESSING: In a blender or using an immersion blender in a wide-mouth jar, combine the dressing ingredients. Blend, starting on low and bringing up the speed, until the dressing is smooth and creamy. Set aside until you're ready to serve. This keeps in the fridge for 3 to 5 days.

ASSEMBLE THE SALAD: In a large bowl, combine the lettuce, cucumbers, tomatoes, red onion, dill, mint, and parsley. Pour the desired amount of dressing over the salad and toss until the lettuce is well coated.

DIVIDE the salad mixture among four plates. Top with the crisped pita and additional feta.

# blt panzanella

**MAKES 4 SERVINGS** • **TOTAL TIME: 35 MINUTES**

DAIRY-FREE

*if modified:*

GLUTEN-FREE

### FOR THE BACON AND CROUTONS

One 10-ounce package no-sugar-added bacon (about 10 slices)

4 cups 1-inch-cubed sourdough or Italian bread (sub gluten-free bread)

2 tablespoons extra-virgin olive oil

¼ teaspoon kosher salt

½ teaspoon dried thyme

### FOR THE HERBY DRESSING

½ cup Homemade Mayo (page 7)

¼ cup finely chopped fresh chives

2 tablespoons freshly squeezed lemon juice (about 1 lemon)

1 tablespoon red wine vinegar

1 teaspoon Dijon mustard

1 garlic clove, minced

½ teaspoon kosher salt

½ teaspoon freshly ground black pepper, plus more for serving

### FOR THE SALAD

6 cups baby arugula

6 Campari tomatoes or tomatoes on the vine, cut into wedges

½ cup halved yellow or red cherry tomatoes

¼ cup torn fresh basil leaves, plus more for serving

*When I was young, my dad introduced me to the simple joy that is a BLT sandwich. Ripe summer tomatoes, fresh bread, lettuce, crisp bacon, mayo, and always, a lot of black pepper. Here, I've combined the elements of a BLT—salty bacon, arugula, and ripe tomatoes—with golden homemade croutons and a creamy, tangy dressing. This is the perfect twist on the popular Tuscan panzanella, a summer salad that comprises soaked stale bread, onions, and tomatoes.*

**COOK THE BACON:** Line a plate with paper towels and set aside. Line a large sheet pan with parchment paper. Arrange the bacon in a single layer on the sheet pan, ensuring the slices do not overlap. Set on an oven rack in the center of a cold oven and turn the temperature to 375°F. Bake until the bacon is just crisp, 25 to 27 minutes. Transfer to the plate lined with paper towels. Set aside.

**WHILE THE BACON IS IN THE OVEN, PREPARE THE CROUTONS:** With about 10 minutes left on the bacon timer, spread the cubed bread on another large sheet pan. Drizzle with the oil, sprinkle with the salt and thyme, and toss until coated. Bake until golden brown, 8 to 10 minutes.

**MEANWHILE, MAKE THE HERBY DRESSING:** In a medium bowl, whisk together the dressing ingredients. Set aside. This keeps in the fridge for 5 to 7 days.

**ASSEMBLE THE SALAD:** Place the arugula in a large bowl. Chop the bacon and add it to the bowl. Add the tomatoes, basil, and desired amount of dressing. Gently toss. Add the croutons and gently toss once more.

**DIVIDE** the salad among four bowls. Top with some additional basil and freshly ground black pepper.

# warm farro steak salad

**MAKES 4 SERVINGS • TOTAL TIME: 35 MINUTES**

### FOR THE FARRO

1½ cups uncooked farro

½ teaspoon kosher salt

### FOR THE DRESSING

¼ cup extra-virgin olive oil

Grated zest of ½ lemon

2 tablespoons freshly squeezed lemon juice (about 1 lemon)

1 tablespoon apple cider vinegar

2 garlic cloves, minced

½ teaspoon dried thyme

½ teaspoon kosher salt

¼ teaspoon freshly ground black pepper

### FOR THE STEAKS

4 filet mignon steaks (6 to 8 ounces each)

1½ teaspoons kosher salt

½ teaspoon freshly ground black pepper

2 tablespoons extra-virgin olive oil

### FOR THE SALAD

6 cups arugula

2 ripe pears, cored and thinly sliced

¾ cup roughly chopped walnuts

½ cup Gorgonzola cheese crumbles (omit for dairy-free)

Freshly ground black pepper, for serving

*In the colder months, sometimes I just don't feel like eating a chilled, crisp salad and that's when recipes like this steak salad come to the rescue! The sweet, nutty flavor of the farro pairs perfectly with toasted walnuts and fresh pear to create a healthy and hearty salad. The juicy, tender steak is just the cherry on top of this simple yet elegant dish.*

**COOK THE FARRO:** In a large saucepan, combine the farro, 3 cups water, and the salt. Bring to a boil. Reduce the heat to a vigorous simmer and cook, uncovered and stirring occasionally, until the farro is chewy and tender, 15 to 20 minutes. Drain off the excess water and set the farro aside in a large bowl. Cover and keep warm while you prepare the rest of the salad.

**MAKE THE DRESSING:** In a medium bowl, whisk together the dressing ingredients. Set aside. This keeps in the fridge for 5 to 7 days.

**PREPARE THE STEAKS:** Pat the steaks very dry with a paper towel, then season both sides of the steak with the salt and pepper.

**IN** a large skillet, preferably cast-iron, heat the oil over medium-high heat. When the oil is shimmering, add the steaks and cook until a deep brown crust has formed and the steaks are cooked to your preferred doneness, 3 to 4 minutes per side for medium-rare, 5 to 6 minutes per side for more well-done. Transfer the steaks to a cutting board and let rest for 10 minutes.

**ASSEMBLE THE SALAD:** To the bowl with the farro, add the arugula, pears, walnuts, and dressing. Gently toss until well coated in the dressing. Divide the salad among four plates.

**THINLY** slice the steaks against the grain and divide the pieces to top the salads. Divide the crumbled Gorgonzola cheese (if using) over each salad and season with some freshly ground black pepper.

# creamy italian chopped salad

MAKES 4 SERVINGS  •  TOTAL TIME: 20 MINUTES

**FOR THE CREAMY ITALIAN DRESSING**

¼ cup Homemade Mayo (page 7)

1 tablespoon freshly squeezed lemon juice (about ½ lemon)

1 tablespoon white wine vinegar

2 teaspoons honey

½ teaspoon Dijon mustard

2 garlic cloves, minced

1 teaspoon dried basil

½ teaspoon dried parsley

½ teaspoon dried thyme

½ teaspoon crushed red pepper flakes

¼ teaspoon kosher salt

½ teaspoon freshly ground black pepper, plus more for serving

**FOR THE SALAD**

4 cups roughly chopped romaine lettuce

4 cups baby arugula

¾ cup halved and thinly sliced red onion (about ½ onion)

1 cup medium-diced Genoa salami (4 ounces)

1 cup medium-diced provolone cheese (omit for dairy-free)

¾ cup thinly sliced pepperoncini, drained

1½ cups halved grape tomatoes

½ cup torn in half and pitted green olives

*Meet my absolute favorite "no cook" lunch and dinner! It's a dreamy combination of all my favorite Italian delights and olive bar favorites, chopped up and tossed together in tangy, creamy homemade Italian dressing. Whether you need a great make-ahead lunch or just want to use up any leftover deli meat at home for an easy dinner, this chopped salad is soon to be your favorite, too.*

**MAKE THE CREAMY ITALIAN DRESSING:** In a blender or using an immersion blender in a wide-mouth jar, combine the dressing ingredients. Blend until smooth and creamy. Set aside. This keeps in the fridge for 5 to 7 days.

**MAKE THE SALAD:** In a large bowl, combine the romaine, arugula, red onion, salami, provolone (if using), pepperoncini, tomatoes, and olives. Drizzle with the desired amount of dressing and toss until well combined. Finish with additional freshly ground black pepper.

# cajun cobb salad with shrimp

**MAKES 4 SERVINGS**  •  **TOTAL TIME: 40 MINUTES**

*A Cobb salad is wonderful in its own right, but when you add the layers of flavor from Cajun blackened shrimp and a Cajun-spiced ranch dressing, it's a total game changer. While this salad is great to make and enjoy on the same night, it is also wonderful for meal prep. Simply load up the salads in airtight food containers instead of bowls and add the dressing right before serving.*

## FOR THE CAJUN SEASONING MIX

1 teaspoon garlic powder

1 teaspoon onion powder

1 teaspoon paprika

1 teaspoon dried oregano

1 teaspoon dried thyme

½ teaspoon cayenne pepper

## FOR THE CAJUN RANCH DRESSING

½ cup Homemade Mayo (page 7)

½ teaspoon kosher salt

½ teaspoon freshly ground black pepper

¼ cup unsweetened full-fat coconut milk

1 tablespoon freshly squeezed lemon juice (about ½ lemon)

1 tablespoon red wine vinegar

2 tablespoons finely chopped fresh chives

## FOR THE SALAD

8 cups thinly sliced romaine lettuce (about 2 medium heads)

1½ cups halved cherry tomatoes

½ cup halved and thinly sliced shallot (about 1 large shallot)

3 hard-boiled eggs, quartered

4 slices no-sugar-added bacon, cooked until crisp and chopped

1 avocado, thinly sliced

## FOR THE SHRIMP

1 pound peeled, deveined, and tail-off shrimp (31/40 count)

1 teaspoon kosher salt

½ teaspoon freshly ground black pepper

2 tablespoons extra-virgin olive oil

1 tablespoon freshly squeezed lemon juice (about ½ lemon)

**MAKE THE CAJUN SEASONING MIX:** In a small bowl, combine the seasoning ingredients. Set aside.

**MAKE THE CAJUN RANCH DRESSING:** In a blender or using an immersion blender in a wide-mouth jar, combine the mayo, salt, black pepper, coconut milk, lemon juice, vinegar, and 2¼ teaspoons of the Cajun seasoning mix. Blend until smooth. Stir in the chives and refrigerate until ready to serve. This keeps in the fridge for 5 to 7 days.

**MAKE THE SALAD:** In a large bowl, combine the romaine, cherry tomatoes, shallot, hard-boiled eggs, chopped bacon, and avocado. Set aside.

**PREPARE THE SHRIMP:** Pat the shrimp very dry with paper towels. Transfer them to a medium bowl and season with the salt, black pepper, and the remaining Cajun seasoning mix. Toss to combine.

**IN** a large skillet, heat the oil over medium-high heat. When the oil is hot but not smoking, transfer the shrimp to the skillet and cook, stirring occasionally, until the shrimp are cooked through and no longer translucent, about 6 minutes. Add the lemon juice to the skillet and toss to combine.

**ADD** the cooked shrimp to the salad and drizzle with the desired amount of the Cajun ranch dressing. Gently toss to coat.

# macho salad

**MAKES 4 SERVINGS** • **TOTAL TIME: 35 MINUTES**

*if modified:*
GLUTEN-FREE
DAIRY-FREE

### FOR THE CROUTONS AND CORN

4 cups 1-inch-cubed ciabatta bread (sub gluten-free bread)

3 tablespoons extra-virgin olive oil, divided

½ teaspoon dried oregano

¼ teaspoon kosher salt

1½ cups frozen corn kernels

### FOR THE DRESSING

¼ cup extra-virgin olive oil

2 tablespoons freshly squeezed lemon juice (about 1 lemon)

1 tablespoon champagne vinegar

1 tablespoon pure maple syrup

2 teaspoons Dijon mustard

1 garlic clove, minced

½ teaspoon dried oregano

½ teaspoon kosher salt

¼ teaspoon freshly ground black pepper

### FOR THE SALAD

3 cups shredded and roughly chopped cooked chicken (I use rotisserie chicken)

8 cups roughly chopped red-leaf lettuce (about 2 medium heads)

¼ cup finely chopped fresh chives

6 Medjool dates, pitted and finely chopped

½ cup thinly sliced shallot (about 1 large shallot)

6 Campari tomatoes or tomatoes on the vine, quartered

1 large avocado, cut into large cubes

3 ounces crumbled goat cheese (omit for dairy-free)

½ cup salted roasted almonds, roughly chopped

Freshly ground black pepper, for serving

*There are a lot of boring, healthy salads out there, but this one is surely not one of those! Inspired by Hillstone's Macho Salad, I've made my own rendition that will leave your tummy full and heart happy! While the original version uses corn bread croutons, I opted to make traditional croutons with store-bought ciabatta bread for the sake of ease. Filled with red lettuce, rotisserie chicken, corn, and, of course, the crunchy croutons, this salad is a meal worth making over and over again!*

PREHEAT the oven to 350°F. Line a large sheet pan with parchment paper.

MAKE THE CROUTONS AND COOK THE CORN: Place the bread on the prepared sheet pan, drizzle with 2 tablespoons of the oil, and season with the dried oregano and salt. Toss to coat and spread into a single layer over half the sheet pan. Pour the frozen corn on the empty half of the pan and drizzle with the remaining 1 tablespoon oil. Toss to coat.

TRANSFER to the oven and bake until the bread is toasted golden brown and crisp and the corn is tender and golden, about 12 minutes. Remove from the oven and set aside.

MEANWHILE, MAKE THE DRESSING: In a small bowl, whisk together the dressing ingredients until well combined. Set aside. This keeps in the fridge for 5 to 7 days.

ASSEMBLE THE SALAD: In a large bowl, combine the chicken and 1 tablespoon of the dressing. Toss well to combine. Add the lettuce, chives, dates, shallot, and the roasted corn. Drizzle with desired amount of additional dressing and toss until well coated. Divide the salad among four bowls.

AROUND the salad greens, divide and scatter the croutons, tomatoes, and avocado. Top with the crumbled goat cheese (if using) and chopped almonds. Season with additional freshly ground black pepper.

# sweet potato fry salad with lemon-tahini dressing

**MAKES 4 SERVINGS** • **TOTAL TIME: 50 MINUTES**

### FOR THE FRIES

2 large unpeeled sweet potatoes, scrubbed and cut into 2-inch-long and ¼-inch-thick fries

¼ cup extra-virgin olive oil

1½ teaspoons kosher salt

1 teaspoon freshly ground black pepper

1 tablespoon za'atar seasoning

### FOR THE LEMON-TAHINI DRESSING

¼ cup tahini

¼ cup extra-virgin olive oil

¼ cup freshly squeezed lemon juice (about 2 lemons)

½ teaspoon kosher salt

½ teaspoon freshly ground black pepper, plus more for serving

3 garlic cloves, minced

3 tablespoons chopped fresh chives

### FOR THE SALAD

8 cups deribbed and thinly sliced lacinato kale (about 2 bunches)

1 large avocado, thinly sliced

¼ cup pomegranate seeds

½ cup freshly shaved parmesan cheese (omit for dairy-free, paleo, and Whole30)

*When dining out, one of my favorite orders is a salad with a side of fries. A big plate of fries is always a win in my opinion, but putting fries on a salad? Even better! Here, za'atar-seasoned sweet potato fries are roasted and piled high on a beautiful bed of lemon-tahini dressed kale. With a little creamy avocado, a bright burst of pomegranate seeds, and some salty shaved parmesan cheese, this salad is straight-up delicious.*

PREHEAT the oven to 425°F. Line two sheet pans with parchment paper.

MAKE THE FRIES: Place the sliced sweet potatoes on the two prepared sheet pans. Evenly distribute the oil, salt, pepper, and za'atar between the two sheet pans. Toss to coat and spread the fries into an even layer on each pan.

BAKE until the potatoes are golden brown and cooked through, about 30 minutes, rotating the sheet pans and tossing the fries halfway through the cook time.

MEANWHILE, MAKE THE LEMON-TAHINI DRESSING: In a small bowl, whisk together the dressing ingredients. Tahini thickness can vary; if the dressing is too thick, add 2 to 4 tablespoons of warm water until it reaches a Caesar dressing consistency. Set aside.

ASSEMBLE THE SALAD: Place the kale in a large bowl. Add the desired amount of dressing (reserving about 2 tablespoons for serving) and toss continuously until the kale is well coated and slightly wilted, 2 to 3 minutes. Divide among four bowls.

DIVIDE the fries evenly among the bowls, placing them in the center. Add the avocado around the fries, then divide the pomegranate seeds and parmesan (if using) over the top. Drizzle with the reserved dressing and season with additional freshly ground black pepper.

# deconstructed waldorf salad

GLUTEN-FREE

GRAIN-FREE

**MAKES 4 SERVINGS** • **TOTAL TIME: 25 MINUTES**

### FOR THE DRESSING

2 tablespoons 2% or whole-milk Greek yogurt

2 tablespoons extra-virgin olive oil

2 tablespoons freshly squeezed lemon juice (about 1 lemon)

1 teaspoon honey

1 teaspoon Dijon mustard

3 garlic cloves, minced

¼ teaspoon dried thyme

¼ teaspoon kosher salt

¼ teaspoon freshly ground black pepper

### FOR THE CHICKEN

1 pound boneless, skinless chicken breasts

1 teaspoon kosher salt

½ teaspoon freshly ground black pepper

½ teaspoon dried thyme

2 tablespoons extra-virgin olive oil

### FOR THE SALAD

6 cups baby arugula

½ cup finely chopped fresh parsley

1 medium green apple, cored and thinly sliced

1 cup halved seedless red grapes

¾ cup roughly chopped walnuts

½ cup crumbled blue cheese

Freshly ground black pepper, for serving

*You are likely familiar with a Waldorf chicken salad—a lunchtime classic. While there are many variations, they generally all contain chopped roasted chicken, grapes, and nuts dressed in a mayonnaise-based dressing. Here, you get to keep everything you love about the classic salad but take it to a whole new level with extra greens and a Greek yogurt dressing. It's the perfect light meal that's likely done in less time than it would take to run to your local salad shop.*

MAKE THE DRESSING: In a small jar or bowl, combine the dressing ingredients. Whisk well until the dressing is smooth. Set aside. This keeps in the fridge for 3 to 5 days.

PREPARE THE CHICKEN: Place the chicken breasts on a cutting board and cover with parchment paper or plastic wrap. Using a meat mallet or the bottom of a heavy skillet, pound the chicken to a uniform ½-inch thickness. Pat dry with paper towels. Season both sides of the chicken with the salt, pepper, and thyme.

IN a large nonstick skillet, heat the oil over medium-high heat. When the skillet is hot, cook the chicken until golden brown on both sides and cooked through, 5 to 7 minutes per side. Transfer the cooked chicken to a clean cutting board. Let the chicken rest for 3 minutes, then cut it against the grain into bite-size pieces.

ASSEMBLE THE SALAD: In a large bowl, arrange the arugula, parsley, apple, grapes, walnuts, blue cheese, and chicken. Drizzle with the desired amount of dressing and toss until well coated. Season with additional freshly ground black pepper.

**46** THE BEST CHICKEN TORTILLA SOUP

**49** EASY ITALIAN WEDDING SOUP

**50** SIMPLE BLACK BEAN SOUP

**53** CURRIED CHILI

**54** CHICKEN POT PIE CHOWDER

**57** GREEN CHILE CHICKEN AND RICE SOUP

**58** AROMATIC SHRIMP AND NOODLE SOUP

**61** ITALIAN LENTIL SOUP

**62** LOADED POTATO LEEK SOUP

**65** GREEN CURRY CHICKEN SOUP

**66** TOMATO-BASIL TORTELLINI AND SAUSAGE SOUP

**68** SLOW COOKER OR PRESSURE COOKER
SPICED BEEF STEW

soups

# the best chicken tortilla soup

**MAKES 6 SERVINGS** • **TOTAL TIME: 45 MINUTES**

2 tablespoons extra-virgin olive oil

1 cup finely diced yellow onion (½ medium onion)

½ cup diced carrots (1 medium carrot)

4 garlic cloves, minced

2 tablespoons tomato paste

½ teaspoon chipotle chile powder (sub smoked paprika for less spice)

2 teaspoons chili powder

½ teaspoon ground cumin

1 teaspoon kosher salt, plus more to taste

½ teaspoon freshly ground black pepper

One 14.5-ounce can diced fire-roasted tomatoes

One 4-ounce can mild diced green chiles

6 cups low-sodium chicken broth

2 tablespoons minced fresh cilantro leaves

2 bay leaves

1½ pounds boneless, skinless chicken breasts

1 cup finely crushed white corn tortilla chips

1 tablespoon freshly squeezed lime juice (about ½ lime)

### FOR SERVING

Shredded Monterey Jack cheese (omit for dairy-free)

1 avocado, thinly sliced

White corn tortilla chips

Chopped fresh cilantro leaves

1 lime, cut into wedges

*Tortilla soup has always been one of my favorite soups to order when dining out at local Tex-Mex restaurants. When ordering the dish at different places, you'll find that tortilla soup really varies. Sometimes it's really thick and creamy and other times very brothy. I like mine somewhere in between—and really think this one is just perfect. The trick? Blend up some of the soup base with white corn tortilla chips! It might sound a little unusual, but this helps thicken the soup slightly and infuses the tortilla flavor into the soup.*

IN a large pot or Dutch oven, heat the oil over medium-high heat. Add the onion, carrots, and garlic and cook, stirring, until the onion is tender, about 5 minutes. Add the tomato paste, chipotle powder, chili powder, cumin, salt, and pepper and continue to cook, stirring, to toast the spices and cook the tomato paste until fragrant, 2 to 3 minutes.

ADD the fire-roasted tomatoes, diced green chiles, chicken broth, cilantro, and bay leaves and bring to a rapid simmer. Carefully lower the chicken breasts into the broth, cover, and cook until the chicken is cooked through, 15 to 20 minutes, depending on the thickness of the chicken.

USING tongs, transfer the chicken breasts to a sheet pan and set aside to cool. Discard the bay leaves. Reduce the heat in the pot to medium-low to keep the soup warm.

LADLE 3 cups of the soup mixture into a blender and add the crushed white corn tortilla chips. Let sit for about 2 minutes for the chips to soften and absorb some of the liquid, then blend until smooth. Pour the mixture back into the pot and stir to combine.

USING two forks, shred the chicken. Return it to the soup, cover, and let everything warm back up and the flavors meld together, about 5 more minutes. Squeeze in the lime juice and stir to combine. Taste and add more salt as desired.

TO SERVE: Ladle the soup into bowls and garnish as desired. I top mine with a sprinkle of Monterey Jack cheese, some sliced avocado, tortilla chips, cilantro, and a squeeze of lime to finish.

# easy italian wedding soup

**MAKES 6 SERVINGS** • **TOTAL TIME: 1 HOUR**

*if modified:*
DAIRY-FREE
GLUTEN-FREE

## FOR THE MEATBALLS

½ pound bulk mild Italian sausage

½ pound ground beef (90/10)

1 large egg, whisked

2 tablespoons grated Parmigiano-Reggiano cheese (omit for dairy-free)

¼ teaspoon kosher salt

¼ teaspoon freshly ground black pepper

2 tablespoons cassava flour (sub plain bread crumbs if not gluten-free)

Grated zest of ½ lemon

2 tablespoons extra-virgin olive oil

## FOR THE SOUP

¾ cup medium-diced celery (about 2 stalks)

¾ cup medium-diced carrot (1 large carrot)

1 cup medium-diced yellow onion (about ½ medium onion)

3 garlic cloves, minced

1 teaspoon kosher salt, plus more to taste

½ teaspoon freshly ground black pepper, plus more to taste

8 cups low-sodium chicken broth

Grated zest of ½ lemon

2 tablespoons freshly squeezed lemon juice (about 1 lemon)

2 tablespoons finely chopped fresh parsley leaves

1 tablespoon finely chopped fresh oregano or 1 teaspoon dried

¾ cup Israeli couscous (sub gluten-free acini di pepe or orzo for gluten-free)

4 cups (about 1 bunch) chopped escarole or deribbed lacinato kale

Grated Parmigiano-Reggiano cheese, for serving (omit for dairy-free)

*For a warm bowl of Italian comfort, wedding soup is one of my absolute favorites. The name comes from the Italian phrase minestra maritata or "married soup," because of the marriage of ingredients that lends to its wonderful flavor. My favorite part about this soup? It has meatballs in it, so it feels like a hearty meal! A touch of Israeli couscous adds creaminess to the soup while still letting the meatballs shine.*

**PREPARE THE MEATBALLS:** In a medium bowl, combine the sausage, ground beef, egg, Parmigiano-Reggiano (if using), salt, pepper, cassava flour, and lemon zest. Using clean hands, mix the meat until well combined, then form the meat mixture into 1-inch balls. Set aside.

**IN** a large pot or Dutch oven, heat the oil over medium-high heat. When the oil is hot, working in batches as needed, place the meatballs in the pot in a single layer and brown on all sides for about 2 minutes per side. The meatballs don't have to be fully cooked through, as they will continue to cook in the soup. When the meatballs are browned, transfer them to a plate.

**PREPARE THE SOUP:** Reduce the heat under the pot to medium. Add the celery, carrot, onion, garlic, salt, and pepper. Cook, stirring and scraping up any browned bits, until the veggies have softened, 4 to 6 minutes. Add the broth, lemon zest, lemon juice, parsley, and oregano.

**BRING** the soup to a light boil. Reduce the soup to a simmer and add the meatballs and couscous. Cook, uncovered, and stirring occasionally, until the couscous is tender and the meatballs are cooked through, about 10 minutes.

**STIR** in the escarole and cook until just tender, about 2 minutes. Taste and adjust the salt and pepper, if desired.

**LADLE** the soup into individual bowls and top with additional Parmigiano-Reggiano (if using).

## FROM MY KITCHEN TO YOURS

**REHEATING TIPS:** When left in the fridge, the couscous will absorb additional broth. Reheat on the stove and add more broth 1 cup at a time as needed.

# simple black bean soup

MAKES 6 SERVINGS  •  TOTAL TIME: 40 MINUTES

4 slices no-sugar-added bacon, diced (omit for vegetarian and sub 2 tablespoons extra virgin olive oil)

3 garlic cloves, minced

1½ cups diced yellow onion (about 1 medium onion)

1 serrano pepper, thinly sliced

1 teaspoon kosher salt, plus more to taste

½ teaspoon freshly ground black pepper

1 tablespoon chili powder

1 teaspoon ground cumin

1 teaspoon paprika

1 teaspoon dried oregano

Four 15-ounce cans low-sodium black beans, drained and rinsed

3 cups low-sodium vegetable broth

1 tablespoon apple cider vinegar

2 bay leaves

1 tablespoon freshly squeezed lime juice (about ½ lime)

¼ cup chopped fresh cilantro leaves

### FOR SERVING

Sour cream or plain Greek yogurt (omit for dairy-free)

Crumbled Cotija cheese (omit for dairy-free)

Crushed tortilla chips (omit for grain-free)

Chopped fresh cilantro

Lime wedges

*I love a meal that relies mostly on pantry staples, and this easy black bean soup is just that. Using canned black beans rather than dried, this soup comes together effortlessly. Although the soup cooks in under an hour, the flavor still has plenty of time to develop, and the soup is filling and hearty enough for a cozy dinner. I blend just a portion of the soup to thicken up the broth a bit for a creamy, decadent texture. It's the perfect weeknight go-to when you haven't gone to the grocery store in a while!*

HEAT a large pot or Dutch oven over medium heat. When hot, add the bacon (if using) and cook, stirring occasionally, until the bacon is crisped, 4 to 5 minutes. To keep vegetarian, heat the oil over medium heat.

ADD the garlic, onion, serrano, salt, and black pepper and sauté until the onion is tender, 4 to 5 minutes.

ADD the chili powder, cumin, paprika, and oregano and continue to cook, stirring, toasting the spices for about 1 minute, until fragrant.

ADD the beans, vegetable broth, and vinegar. Stir to combine. Add the bay leaves and bring to a boil. Reduce the heat to a simmer, cover, and cook until the beans have softened and the flavors have melded, 15 to 20 minutes.

DISCARD the bay leaves. Transfer about 2 cups of the soup to a high-powered blender and blend until mostly smooth. Carefully pour the pureed beans back into the pot and stir to combine.

ADD the lime juice and cilantro. Taste and add more salt if needed. Stir to combine and simmer, uncovered, for 5 more minutes.

DIVIDE the soup among bowls. If using, top with sour cream, Cotija, and tortilla chips. Add a sprinkle of cilantro and serve with a lime wedge.

# curried chili

**MAKES 4 SERVINGS** • **TOTAL TIME: 45 MINUTES**

GLUTEN-FREE

GRAIN-FREE

*if modified:*
DAIRY-FREE
PALEO
WHOLE30

## FOR THE CHILI

2 tablespoons extra-virgin olive oil

2 cups diced yellow onion (about 1 medium onion)

1 medium jalapeño, seeded and finely diced

2 garlic cloves, minced

2 pounds ground beef (90/10)

1-inch piece fresh ginger, peeled and finely grated

4 teaspoons curry powder

1 teaspoon ground cumin

½ teaspoon ground coriander

½ teaspoon ground turmeric

½ teaspoon smoked paprika

¼ teaspoon cayenne pepper, optional

1½ teaspoons kosher salt

1 teaspoon freshly ground black pepper

One 14.5-ounce can diced tomatoes

One 15-ounce can tomato sauce

½ cup low-sodium beef broth

One 15-ounce can chickpeas, drained and rinsed (omit for paleo and Whole30)

## FOR SERVING

¼ cup sour cream or plain Greek yogurt, optional (omit for dairy-free, paleo, and Whole30)

¼ cup golden raisins, roughly chopped, optional

¼ cup fresh cilantro leaves, optional

Freshly ground black pepper, optional

1 lime, cut into wedges

*Here is a new take on a classic, cozy pot of chili that I cannot get enough of. This curried chili is a fusion recipe that combines Tex-Mex chili with the flavors of an Indian curry. It's got the perfect amount of spice, is bursting with flavor, and is so easy to make! Its unique and deep flavor develops quickly. But the best part about this recipe, as with any chili, is that it just keeps getting better each day, making it perfect for meal prep!*

IN a large pot or Dutch oven, heat the oil over medium-high heat. Add the onion, jalapeño, and garlic. Cook, stirring, until the onion is tender, about 4 minutes.

ADD the ground beef and grated ginger and cook, breaking up the meat with the edge of a spoon, until the meat is cooked through and no longer pink, about 8 minutes. Drain off excess fat, if needed.

ADD the curry powder, cumin, coriander, turmeric, smoked paprika, cayenne (if using), salt, and black pepper and continue to cook, toasting the spices until fragrant, about 2 minutes.

ADD the diced tomatoes, tomato sauce, and beef broth and stir to combine. Bring the chili to a boil, then reduce the heat to low for a light simmer. Cover and cook to let the flavors meld, about 20 minutes, stirring occasionally.

ADD the chickpeas (if using) and stir to combine. Cover and cook until the chickpeas are tender, about 10 more minutes.

TO SERVE: Ladle the chili into bowls. If desired, top with a dollop of sour cream, a few golden raisins, cilantro, and additional freshly ground black pepper. Serve with a wedge of lime.

# chicken pot pie chowder

**MAKES 6 SERVINGS** • **TOTAL TIME: 40 MINUTES**

2 tablespoons extra-virgin olive oil

1½ cups medium-diced carrot (about 3 medium carrots)

1 cup medium-diced celery (about 2 stalks)

1 cup small-diced yellow onion (about ½ medium onion)

2 garlic cloves, minced

1½ teaspoons kosher salt, plus more to taste

½ teaspoon freshly ground black pepper, plus more for serving (optional)

2 cups thinly sliced baby bella mushrooms

2 tablespoons arrowroot or tapioca flour

4 cups low-sodium chicken broth

1 cup unsweetened full-fat coconut milk

2 cups medium-diced unpeeled Yukon Gold potatoes (about ½ pound)

2 teaspoons fresh thyme leaves or 1 teaspoon dried, plus more fresh thyme for serving (optional)

1 bay leaf

¼ teaspoon cayenne pepper

2½ cups diced cooked chicken (I use a rotisserie chicken)

1 cup frozen peas

2 tablespoons finely chopped fresh parsley

Grated zest of ½ lemon

1 tablespoon freshly squeezed lemon juice (about ½ lemon)

*To me, there is nothing more comforting than a chicken pot pie. The flavors always take me straight back to my childhood when my mom would prepare the classic—albeit often frozen—deliciousness. This soup has all the comforts of a classic chicken pot pie made in one pot but without the crust. Have all your ingredients chopped and ready to go and this soup will come together very easily. It's an instant family favorite.*

IN a large pot or Dutch oven, heat the oil over medium heat. Add the carrots, celery, onion, garlic, salt, and black pepper and cook, stirring, until the veggies are tender, about 5 minutes. Stir in the mushrooms and sauté for an additional 2 minutes.

REDUCE the heat to medium. Add the arrowroot flour and stir until well combined with the vegetables. Continue stirring and slowly pour in the chicken broth, scraping up any browned bits on the bottom of the skillet.

ADD the coconut milk, potatoes, thyme, bay leaf, and cayenne and stir to combine. Bring the soup to a boil. Reduce the heat to a light simmer, cover, and cook, simmering, until the potatoes are fork-tender, about 12 minutes.

ADD the chicken, peas, parsley, lemon zest, and lemon juice. Stir until well combined. Simmer, uncovered, until the peas are thawed, about 4 minutes. Taste and adjust the salt as desired. Discard the bay leaf.

SERVE in bowls topped with fresh thyme leaves and additional freshly ground black pepper, if desired.

# green chile chicken and rice soup

GLUTEN-FREE

DAIRY-FREE

**MAKES 6 SERVINGS • TOTAL TIME: 40 MINUTES**

2 tablespoons extra-virgin olive oil

2 cups small-diced yellow onion (about 1 medium onion)

½ cup seeded and finely diced jalapeño (about 1 large jalapeño)

4 garlic cloves, minced

1 teaspoon kosher salt, plus more to taste

1 teaspoon freshly ground black pepper, plus more to taste

1½ pounds boneless, skinless chicken breasts, halved crosswise

One 15-ounce can mild green enchilada sauce

4 cups low-sodium chicken broth

Two 4-ounce cans mild diced green chiles

½ teaspoon ground cumin

½ teaspoon dried oregano

½ cup basmati rice

1 tablespoon freshly squeezed lime juice (about ½ lime)

¼ cup chopped fresh cilantro leaves, plus more for serving

### OPTIONAL FOR SERVING

6 radishes, cut into thin matchsticks

1 large avocado, thinly sliced

Tortilla chips, crumbled

1 lime, cut into wedges

*When I was growing up, my mom made a delicious green chile chicken and rice casserole that I absolutely loved. Borrowing the flavors from that nostalgic meal, I've made a cozy bowl of soup that couldn't be easier to make. Other than dicing up the onion and jalapeño at the beginning, this is a simple throw-in-the-pot soup where magic happens with very little effort! This is bound to become a go-to on your busy weeknights.*

IN a large pot or Dutch oven, heat the oil over medium heat. Add the onion, jalapeño, garlic, salt, and black pepper. Cook, stirring, until the onion is tender, about 6 minutes.

ADD the chicken, enchilada sauce, broth, green chiles, cumin, and oregano and stir to combine. Bring the soup to a boil.

REDUCE the heat to a light simmer. Stir in the rice, cover, and simmer until the chicken is fully cooked through and the rice is tender, about 20 minutes.

USING tongs, transfer the chicken to a clean cutting board and let cool slightly before cutting it into ½-inch cubes. Return the cubed chicken to the soup and stir to combine. Add the lime juice and cilantro. Taste and adjust the seasoning, if desired.

SERVE in bowls. If desired, top with garnishes. I add radish, cilantro, avocado, and crushed tortilla chips to mine and serve with a wedge of lime.

### FROM MY KITCHEN TO YOURS

REHEATING TIPS: When left in the fridge, the rice will absorb additional broth. Reheat on the stove and add more broth 1 cup at a time as needed.

# aromatic shrimp and noodle soup

**MAKES 4 SERVINGS** • **TOTAL TIME: 25 MINUTES**

## FOR THE SOUP

2 tablespoons avocado oil

1 teaspoon toasted sesame oil

3 garlic cloves, thinly sliced

1-inch piece fresh ginger, peeled and cut into very thin matchsticks

½ cup halved and thinly sliced yellow onion (about ½ medium onion)

4 green onions, halved lengthwise and cut crosswise into 2-inch lengths, white and green parts kept separate

1 teaspoon kosher salt

½ teaspoon Chinese five-spice powder

6 cups seafood stock or low-sodium chicken broth

2 teaspoons fish sauce (I use Red Boat brand)

2 tablespoons coconut aminos

2 tablespoons no-sugar-added sriracha

¼ cup finely chopped fresh cilantro leaves and tender stems

Grated zest of ½ lime

1 lemongrass stalk

8 ounces rice noodles

1 pound peeled, deveined, tails-off shrimp (31/40 count)

## FOR SERVING

2 cups mung bean sprouts

Fresh cilantro leaves, roughly chopped

Fresh Thai basil leaves, torn

1 jalapeño, thinly sliced, optional

No-sugar-added sriracha, for drizzling

1 lime, cut into wedges

*Inspired by the flavors of pho, this soup is filled with beautiful aromatics like ginger, garlic, and Chinese five-spice for a quick take on the Vietnamese classic noodle soup. This fragrant broth is finished with quickly poached shrimp and ladled over prepared rice noodles. Topped with bean sprouts, lime, and, of course, lots of fresh herbs, this steamy bowl of soup is sure to satisfy.*

IN a large pot or Dutch oven, heat the avocado oil and sesame oil over medium heat. Add the garlic, ginger, yellow onion, white parts of the green onion, and the salt. Cook, stirring, until tender, about 3 minutes. Add the five-spice powder and stir until fragrant and toasted, about 1 minute.

STIR in the stock, fish sauce, coconut aminos, sriracha, cilantro, and lime zest.

USING the back of your knife, carefully pound the lemongrass on a cutting board, bruising it to release the flavor. Add it to the soup and bring it to a boil. Reduce the heat to a gentle simmer, cover, and cook while you prepare the rice noodles.

IN a separate pot, prepare the rice noodles according to the package directions. Drain and rinse them under cold water. Set aside.

BRING the broth back to a rapid simmer. Add the shrimp and green portion of the green onions and stir to combine. Simmer, uncovered, until the shrimp are pink and cooked through, about 3 minutes. Remove from the heat.

TO SERVE: Divide the rice noodles among four bowls. Ladle the shrimp and broth over the noodles. Top each bowl with bean sprouts, cilantro, basil, and jalapeño (if using). Add a drizzle of sriracha. Serve with a wedge of lime.

# italian lentil soup

GLUTEN-FREE

VEGETARIAN

*if modified:*
DAIRY-FREE

2 tablespoons extra-virgin olive oil, plus more for serving

1 cup finely chopped yellow onion (about 1 medium onion)

¾ cup finely chopped celery (about 2 stalks)

¾ cup finely chopped carrot (about 2 small carrots)

4 garlic cloves, minced

2 teaspoons kosher salt, plus more to taste

1 teaspoon freshly ground black pepper, plus more for serving

½ teaspoon crushed red pepper flakes

1 teaspoon Italian seasoning

1½ cups brown or green lentils, rinsed

½ cup dry white wine

8 cups low-sodium vegetable broth

One 14.5-ounce can diced fire-roasted tomatoes

10 fresh thyme sprigs (tied into a bundle with kitchen twine) or 1 teaspoon dried thyme

1 bay leaf

1 parmesan cheese rind (omit for dairy-free)

4 cups deribbed and roughly chopped lacinato kale (about 1 bunch)

2 tablespoons freshly squeezed lemon juice (about 1 lemon)

¼ cup finely chopped fresh basil leaves

Freshly grated parmesan cheese, for serving (omit for dairy-free)

*My Italian mother made a version of this lentil soup often when I was growing up and it was full of zesty Italian flavors and lots of fresh veggies. Similar to a minestrone, this soup has an added protein boost from the lentils! And what I love most is that this soup relies heavily on pantry and fridge staples, making it the perfect cozy-comfort food for days you do not have time to get to the grocery store.*

IN a large pot or Dutch oven, heat the oil over medium-high heat. Add the onion, celery, carrot, garlic, salt, black pepper, pepper flakes, and Italian seasoning. Cook, stirring, until tender, 5 to 7 minutes.

ADD the lentils and stir to combine. Pour in the wine and cook until reduced by half, about 2 minutes.

ADD the broth, diced tomatoes, thyme, bay leaf, and parmesan cheese rind (if using). Stir to combine. Bring to a rapid simmer, then reduce the heat to a light simmer. Cover and cook until the lentils are tender, about 25 minutes, stirring occasionally.

ADD the kale and stir to combine. Cover and cook until the kale has wilted and is tender, about 5 minutes.

DISCARD the bundle of thyme, bay leaf, and cheese rind. Add the lemon juice and basil. Stir to combine. Taste and add more salt, if desired.

LADLE the soup into bowls to serve. Add a drizzle of oil, additional freshly ground black pepper, and the grated parmesan (if using).

GLUTEN-FREE

GRAIN-FREE

*if modified:*

DAIRY-FREE

PALEO

WHOLE30

VEGETARIAN

# loaded potato leek soup

**MAKES 6 SERVINGS** • **TOTAL TIME: 40 MINUTES**

6 slices no-sugar-added bacon, diced (omit for vegetarian and sub 2 tablespoons extra virgin olive oil)

2 cups diced yellow onion (about 1 medium onion)

3 large leeks, white and light-green parts only, roughly chopped (about 5 cups), well rinsed (see note)

6 garlic cloves, roughly chopped

2 teaspoons kosher salt, plus more to taste

1 teaspoon freshly ground black pepper, plus more for serving

2½ pounds Yukon Gold potatoes, unpeeled, cut into ½-inch cubes

6 cups low-sodium vegetable broth

1 cup unsweetened full-fat coconut milk

2 bay leaves

1 teaspoon dried thyme

2 tablespoons freshly squeezed lemon juice (about 1 lemon)

### FOR SERVING

½ cup finely chopped fresh chives

½ cup freshly grated medium-sharp cheddar cheese (omit for dairy-free, paleo, and Whole30)

*I love nothing more than a good potato soup—or, let's be real, a potato in any form. This soup combines two of my favorites: a loaded baked potato and a potato leek soup. Creamy, warm, filling, and healthy, this is a soup your family will beg you to make every week. And, not to mention, the whole house will smell wonderful as it cooks.*

LINE a plate with paper towels (if using bacon). Add the bacon to a large pot or Dutch oven. Set the pan over medium heat and cook, tossing occasionally, until just crisp and the fat has rendered, about 7 minutes. Using a slotted spoon, transfer the cooked bacon to the plate lined with paper towels and set aside, reserving the bacon fat in the pot. To keep vegetarian, heat the olive oil over medium heat.

ADD the onion, leeks, garlic, salt, and pepper to the pot and cook, stirring, until the vegetables are tender, about 7 minutes.

ADD the potatoes, broth, coconut milk, bay leaves, and thyme. Stir to combine and bring the soup to a boil. Reduce the heat to a light simmer, cover, and cook until the potatoes are fork-tender, 15 to 20 minutes. Discard the bay leaves.

USING an immersion blender, blend the soup until just smooth. (Alternatively, you can carefully transfer the soup, in batches, to a high-powered blender and blend until smooth.) Stir in the lemon juice and add salt to taste.

SERVE in bowls and top with the reserved bacon bits (if using), chives, cheddar (if using), and additional freshly ground black pepper.

### FROM MY KITCHEN TO YOURS

Leeks can be very dirty; you need to clean them very well inside and out to remove any sediment so you do not get any grittiness in your soup. I've found the best way to clean them is to place the sliced leeks in a colander and run hot water over them until they are well rinsed. Place the leeks on paper towels and pat them dry until ready to use.

# green curry chicken soup

**MAKES 6 SERVINGS** • **TOTAL TIME: 30 MINUTES**

2 tablespoons avocado oil

½ cup diced shallot (about 1 large shallot)

3 garlic cloves, minced

1-inch piece fresh ginger, peeled and finely grated

2 cups stemmed and thinly sliced shiitake mushrooms

¼ cup Thai green curry paste (I use Mae Ploy brand)

6 cups low-sodium chicken broth

2 cups unsweetened full-fat coconut milk

2 tablespoons coconut aminos

1 tablespoon fish sauce (I use Red Boat brand)

Grated zest of ½ lime

2 tablespoons freshly squeezed lime juice (about 1 lime)

1 tablespoon coconut sugar

1½ pounds boneless, skinless chicken breasts, thinly sliced

2 heads baby bok choy, roughly chopped

### FOR SERVING

8 ounces rice noodles

Fresh Thai basil leaves, julienned

Fresh cilantro leaves and tender stems, roughly chopped

2 green onions (green parts only), thinly sliced

1 lime, cut into wedges

*There is nothing quite like a bowl of chicken soup. It's one of those things that you turn to when you're fighting a cold or when you're just craving something cozy and nostalgic. This Thai-inspired take on the classic features a kick of spice from green curry paste, creaminess from coconut milk, and a nice hint of brightness from the lime juice and zest. It's a fun one to make anytime you're needing a little chicken soup pick-me-up!*

BRING a medium saucepan of water to a boil (this is for cooking the rice noodles later).

MEANWHILE, in a large pot or Dutch oven, heat the oil over medium heat. Add the shallot, garlic, and ginger and cook, stirring, until the veggies are tender, about 2 minutes.

ADD the mushrooms and continue to cook, stirring, until the mushrooms are slightly tender, about 2 minutes. Add the green curry paste and stir until well combined. Continue stirring and slowly pour in the broth. Add the coconut milk, coconut aminos, fish sauce, lime zest, lime juice, and coconut sugar. Stir to combine.

INCREASE the heat to medium-high and bring the soup to a simmer. Add the sliced chicken, cover, and let simmer until the chicken is cooked through, 8 to 10 minutes. Stir in the bok choy greens.

TO SERVE: Right before serving, add the rice noodles to the pan of boiling water and cook according to the package directions.

LADLE the soup into each bowl. Place a "nest" of rice noodles into the broth. Top with Thai basil, cilantro, and green onions. Serve with a wedge of lime.

# tomato-basil tortellini and sausage soup

**MAKES 4 SERVINGS** • **TOTAL TIME: 35 MINUTES**

2 tablespoons extra-virgin olive oil

1 pound bulk mild or hot Italian sausage

1 cup small-diced yellow onion (about ½ medium onion)

2 garlic cloves, minced

1½ teaspoons kosher salt

½ teaspoon freshly ground black pepper, plus more for serving (optional)

1½ teaspoons Italian seasoning

4 tablespoons tomato paste

One 14.5-ounce can crushed tomatoes

4 cups low-sodium vegetable broth

1 cup unsweetened full-fat coconut milk

¼ cup chopped fresh basil leaves

4 cups deribbed and roughly chopped lacinato kale (about 1 bunch)

One 9-ounce package nondairy cheese tortellini (I use Kite Hill brand)

*This soup is for my sister, Madison. She is a hardworking mom of three young kids and requested a tortellini soup for busy weeknights. Full of Italian sausage, kale, tortellini, basil—and a touch of creaminess from coconut milk for good measure—this is the perfect dairy-free comfort meal. You might as well go ahead and add this on your weekly rotation, because this simple soup is one that the whole family will ask for over and over again!*

IN a large pot or Dutch oven, heat the oil over medium-high heat. Add the sausage and cook, breaking up the meat with the edge of a spoon, until cooked through and no longer pink, 5 to 7 minutes. Drain off all but about 2 tablespoons fat from the pot.

ADD the onion, garlic, salt, pepper, and Italian seasoning. Cook, stirring, until the onion is tender, about 4 minutes.

ADD the tomato paste and stir to combine. Add the crushed tomatoes, vegetable broth, coconut milk, and basil. Stir to combine and bring to a rapid simmer. Reduce the heat to a light simmer and let cook, uncovered and stirring occasionally, for about 5 minutes.

STIR in the kale and tortellini. Continue to cook, uncovered, until the tortellini are tender and the kale has wilted, about 4 more minutes.

REMOVE from heat and serve with additional freshly ground black pepper, if desired.

## FROM MY KITCHEN TO YOURS

If you plan on making this in advance, make the soup base, but do not add the kale or the tortellini. When heating up to serve, simply bring to a simmer, add the kale and tortellini, and cook for 4 minutes, until the pasta is tender and the kale has wilted. When stored, the tortellini will absorb some of the liquid, so add more broth as needed when reheating.

# slow cooker or pressure cooker spiced beef stew

**MAKES 4 SERVINGS** • **TOTAL TIME: 1 HOUR 15 MINUTES OR 8 TO 10 HOURS**

2 pounds beef round or chuck roast, trimmed of excess fat and cut into 2-inch cubes

2 teaspoons kosher salt, divided, plus more to taste

1 teaspoon freshly ground black pepper

2 tablespoons tapioca flour

2 tablespoons extra-virgin olive oil

2 cups medium-diced yellow onion (about 1 medium onion)

1½ cups sliced carrots (about 2 medium carrots)

4 garlic cloves, minced

1 teaspoon ground turmeric

1 teaspoon saffron threads, crumbled

1 teaspoon ground cumin

½ teaspoon ground allspice

¼ teaspoon cayenne pepper, optional

2 tablespoons tomato paste

3 cups low-sodium beef broth

¼ cup mild harissa sauce (I use Mina brand)

1 tablespoon Dijon mustard

1 tablespoon apple cider vinegar

One 14.5-ounce can diced fire-roasted tomatoes

2 cups 1-inch-cubed peeled russet potatoes (about 2 potatoes)

Grated zest of ½ lemon

1 tablespoon freshly squeezed lemon juice (about ½ lemon)

¼ cup finely chopped fresh parsley leaves, plus more for garnish

¼ cup finely chopped fresh dill, plus more for garnish

*I love nothing more than walking through the door after a hectic day with dinner in the slow cooker ready to be eaten. This Middle Eastern–inspired beef stew is a great variation on a classic beef stew. It still offers the comfort we love, but it's a little more fragrant, bold, and exciting. Don't let the wide array of spices make you hesitant about making this for your entire family—my kids love this one as much as I do!*

### FOR BOTH METHODS

PAT the meat very dry with paper towels and transfer it to a large bowl. Season it with 1½ teaspoons of the salt, the black pepper, and tapioca flour. Toss to coat the meat evenly.

IN a large skillet, heat the oil over medium-high heat. Add the beef in a single layer and brown it on all sides, about 2 minutes per side. You will likely need to do this in batches to ensure you do not overcrowd the skillet and the beef gets a nice sear. Transfer the browned beef to a plate and set aside.

TO the skillet with the remaining beef fat, add the onion, carrots, and garlic and sauté until the onions are translucent, about 3 minutes. Add the turmeric, saffron, cumin, allspice, cayenne (if using), the remaining ½ teaspoon salt, and the tomato paste. Stir to combine and toast until fragrant, about 1 minute.

### SLOW COOKER METHOD

TRANSFER the contents of the skillet to the slow cooker along with the beef and any of its juices. Add the beef broth, harissa, mustard, vinegar, diced tomatoes, and potatoes. Stir until very well combined. Cover and cook on low for 8 to 10 hours, until the meat is fork-tender.

WHEN the cook time is complete, stir in the lemon zest, lemon juice, parsley, and dill. Taste and adjust the seasoning as needed.

SERVE in bowls topped with additional parsley and dill, if desired.

## PRESSURE COOKER METHOD

TRANSFER the contents of the skillet to the pressure cooker along with the beef and any of its juices. Add the beef broth, harissa, mustard, vinegar, diced tomatoes, and potatoes. Stir until very well combined. Lock the lid on the pressure cooker and turn the vent to "seal." Press the "meat/stew" button. Let cook for 35 minutes. Once the cook time is finished, allow the pressure cooker to naturally release pressure for 10 minutes before quick-releasing the remaining pressure.

WHEN all the pressure has been released, carefully remove the lid and stir in the lemon zest, lemon juice, parsley, and dill. Taste and adjust the seasoning as needed.

SERVE in bowls topped with additional parsley and dill, if desired.

72  ONE-POT BUTTERNUT SQUASH AND
SAUSAGE PASTA

75  ROASTED SHRIMP, CHERRY TOMATO,
AND FETA PASTA

76  2 A.M. KIMCHI NOODLES

79  HERBY HARISSA LAMB PASTA

80  ONE-SKILLET LASAGNA

83  CREAMY GOAT CHEESE PASTA WITH
SPINACH AND ARTICHOKES

84  ONE-POT GREEN CURRY VEGGIE NOODLES

87  SUN-DRIED TOMATO, PESTO, AND MINT PASTA

88  CREAMY DIJON PENNE WITH KIELBASA

91  BEEF AND BROCCOLI LO MEIN

92  CALABRIAN CHILE PASTA POMODORO

95  TARRAGON MUSHROOM ORZO-TTO

**pasta and noodles**

# one-pot butternut squash and sausage pasta

**MAKES 6 SERVINGS** • **TOTAL TIME: 35 MINUTES**

2 tablespoons extra-virgin olive oil

¼ cup minced shallot (about 1 large shallot)

2 garlic cloves, minced

1 pound bulk hot or mild Italian sausage

½ cup julienned fresh sage leaves

12 ounces brown rice shell pasta (I use Jovial brand)

½ cup dry white wine

2¾ cups low-sodium chicken broth

One 15-ounce can butternut squash puree (sub unsweetened canned pumpkin puree)

1 cup unsweetened full-fat coconut milk

1 teaspoon kosher salt

1 teaspoon freshly ground black pepper, plus more for garnish

½ cup chopped fresh parsley, optional for serving

*Using minimal ingredients, this dairy-free pasta results in the creamiest, most decadent one-pot pasta. The flavors of butternut squash, Italian sausage, and sage blend together beautifully. The final product is like an elegant, adult version of shells and cheese we all grew up loving. Just try it out for yourself—and be prepared to have your mind blown!*

IN a large pot, heat the oil over medium heat. Add the shallot and garlic and sauté until tender, about 2 minutes.

ADD the sausage and sage and cook, breaking up the meat with the edge of a spoon, until it is browned and cooked through, 5 to 6 minutes. Drain off all but about 2 tablespoons of the fat from the pot.

ADD the pasta, wine, chicken broth, butternut squash puree, coconut milk, salt, and pepper and stir to combine. Bring to a gentle simmer but do not boil. Continue to cook, uncovered and stirring often, until the pasta is al dente and the liquid is absorbed and creamy, 13 to 15 minutes. In the beginning, the sauce will look too thin. As the pasta continues to cook, it will release starch that helps make the sauce thick and creamy. When the pasta is al dente and the sauce has thickened, remove the pot from heat and let the pasta rest for about 2 minutes, stirring occasionally.

PLATE and garnish with freshly ground black pepper and fresh parsley, if desired.

## FROM MY KITCHEN TO YOURS

If you cannot find canned butternut squash and are using the canned pumpkin, it will not taste like a pumpkin pie, I promise! Also, this won't work with any gluten-free pastas other than brown rice pasta. Gluten-free pastas made with chickpeas or other legumes will not have enough starch to help thicken the sauce.

# roasted shrimp, cherry tomato, and feta pasta

GLUTEN-FREE

**MAKES 4 SERVINGS** • **TOTAL TIME: 40 MINUTES**

1 pound peeled, deveined, and tails-off shrimp (31/35 count)

3 tablespoons extra-virgin olive oil, divided

Kosher salt and freshly ground black pepper

3 garlic cloves, thinly sliced

¾ cup halved and thinly sliced shallot (about 2 large shallots)

4 cups cherry tomatoes (or 2 pints)

½ teaspoon crushed red pepper flakes, plus more for serving

1 teaspoon paprika

1 teaspoon dried oregano

Grated zest of ½ lemon

¼ cup dry white wine

One 8-ounce block feta cheese, broken into 8 chunks

12 ounces gluten-free fusilli pasta (I use Jovial brown rice pasta)

½ cup julienned basil leaves, plus more for serving

*I am sure you've all seen the viral "baked feta pasta" TikTok trend. It's a very simple recipe that combines cherry tomatoes and a block of feta, roasted in the oven until the cherry tomatoes burst open and the cheese melts. It results in a delicious, creamy sauce. With inspiration from the trend, I've created a rendition that includes roasted shrimp, white wine, some beautiful spices, shallots, and herbs to make an easy, elevated pasta dish that is sure to impress on a busy weeknight.*

PREHEAT the oven to 425°F. Bring a large pot of water to a boil for the pasta.

IN a medium bowl, toss the shrimp with 1 tablespoon of the oil, ¼ teaspoon salt, and ¼ teaspoon black pepper until well combined. Set aside.

IN a 9 × 13-inch baking dish, combine the garlic, shallot, tomatoes, ¾ teaspoon salt, ¼ teaspoon black pepper, the pepper flakes, paprika, oregano, lemon zest, wine, and remaining 2 tablespoons oil. Toss to combine. Nestle the chunks of feta into the tomato mixture. Bake until the cherry tomatoes burst and the feta just begins to melt, about 17 minutes.

MEANWHILE, when the water comes to a boil, add plenty of salt (I use 1 tablespoon) and cook the pasta according to the package directions.

REMOVE the tomato and feta mixture from the oven and stir to combine, letting the feta and tomatoes mix together and start to form a sauce. Add the shrimp, toss to combine, and spread into a single layer. Return to the oven and bake until the shrimp is cooked through, 5 to 7 minutes. The shrimp should be opaque and pink.

REMOVE from the oven. Drain the pasta, add it and the basil to the baking dish, and toss gently until the pasta is very well coated in the creamy sauce.

SERVE with additional pepper flakes, basil, and freshly ground black pepper.

# 2 a.m. kimchi noodles

**MAKES 2 SERVINGS** • **TOTAL TIME: 20 MINUTES**

8 ounces linguine (sub gluten-free pasta for gluten-free)

Kosher salt

2 tablespoons avocado oil

2 teaspoons toasted sesame oil

½ pound boneless, skinless chicken thighs, diced small

½ teaspoon freshly ground black pepper

2 garlic cloves, minced

4 green onions, thinly sliced, white and green parts kept separate

2 tablespoons gochujang (I use Mother In Law's brand; sub a gluten-free brand for gluten-free, see page 6)

1 cup kimchi, roughly chopped (I use Wildbrine brand)

¼ cup coconut aminos

1 tablespoon freshly squeezed lime juice (about ½ lime)

1 tablespoon toasted sesame seeds

*One night at 2 a.m., my husband, Clayton, and I had just gotten home from an event where we'd had a few too many beers, and we were ravenous. I dove into my fridge and pantry and made these simple, saucy, Korean-inspired noodles. We fell madly in love with this delicious recipe, and I hope you will, too—whatever the time of day! This recipe works best if you prep your ingredients before you get started cooking. It all comes together quickly!*

BRING a large pot of water to a boil. Add the linguine and 1 tablespoon of salt to the boiling water and cook according to the package directions. Reserve ½ cup of the pasta water and drain the pasta. Set aside.

IN a large deep skillet, heat the avocado oil and sesame oil over medium-high heat. Add the chicken in a single layer and season with ½ teaspoon salt and the pepper. Cook the chicken until golden brown and cooked through, about 4 minutes per side.

ADD the garlic and white parts of the green onion to the skillet and cook, stirring, until the onion begins to soften, about 2 minutes. Add the gochujang and toss to coat the chicken and veggies. Add the kimchi and coconut aminos. Stir until well combined.

REDUCE the heat to medium-low. Add the pasta to the skillet and using tongs, toss until well coated in the sauce. Pour in the lime juice and about ¼ cup pasta water and continue to toss the noodles until they are well coated and glossy. If the noodles seem dry, add the remaining ¼ cup pasta water and toss once more until well coated.

TO SERVE: Garnish with the green parts of the green onions and the toasted sesame seeds.

# herby harissa lamb pasta

**MAKES 4 SERVINGS** • **TOTAL TIME: 30 MINUTES**

*if modified:*
GLUTEN-FREE

Kosher salt

12 ounces casarecce, strozzapreti, or gemelli pasta (sub brown rice pasta for gluten-free)

2 tablespoons extra-virgin olive oil

1 cup halved and thinly sliced shallots (about 2 large shallots)

2 garlic cloves, minced

½ teaspoon crushed red pepper flakes

1 pound ground lamb (sub ground beef, 90/10)

½ teaspoon freshly ground black pepper

2 tablespoons tomato paste

½ cup mild harissa sauce (I use Mina brand)

½ cup dry white wine

1 cup frozen peas

4 ounces goat cheese

Grated zest of ½ lemon

FOR SERVING

Extra-virgin olive oil, for drizzling

½ cup chopped fresh mint leaves

½ cup chopped fresh dill fronds

1 lemon, cut into wedges

Crushed red pepper flakes, optional

*Here we're adding a Middle Eastern twist to a classic pasta and meat sauce by using spicy harissa and lamb to amp up this deliciously simple recipe. Store-bought harissa adds lots of flavor while the goat cheese adds creaminess and a lovely pop of tang to the sauce. Topped off with mint and dill, this dinner is a perfect way to elevate your pasta game.*

BRING a large pot of water to a boil. Add 1 tablespoon kosher salt and the pasta and cook until al dente according to the package directions.

MEANWHILE, in a large, deep skillet, heat the oil over medium heat. When shimmering, add the shallots, garlic, and pepper flakes and sauté until the shallots are tender, about 3 minutes.

ADD the lamb and cook, breaking the meat up with the edge of a spoon, until the lamb is browned and cooked through, about 7 minutes.

DRAIN off the excess fat, then reduce the heat to medium. Add 1½ teaspoons kosher salt, the black pepper, tomato paste, and harissa. Cook, stirring occasionally, until the spices are fragrant and the tomato paste is cooked down and well combined with the lamb mixture, 1 to 2 minutes.

ADD the wine and cook, stirring, until reduced by half, about 2 minutes. Stir in the frozen peas and let them thaw, about 2 minutes. Reduce the heat to low until the pasta is ready.

WHEN the pasta is cooked, reserve 1 cup of the starchy pasta water and drain the pasta. Add the pasta to the skillet along with the goat cheese and lemon zest, tossing constantly. While tossing, add ¼ cup pasta water at a time until the pasta is well coated in the sauce and glossy. You likely will not need all the pasta water; I usually end up using ½ to ¾ cup.

TO SERVE: Divide the pasta among four bowls and drizzle with a small amount of the oil. Garnish each bowl generously with mint and dill. Serve with a wedge of lemon and more pepper flakes, if desired.

# one-skillet lasagna

**MAKES 6 SERVINGS** • **TOTAL TIME: 45 MINUTES**

2 tablespoons extra-virgin olive oil

½ cup small-diced yellow onion (about ½ small onion)

2 garlic cloves, minced

½ pound ground beef (90/10)

½ pound bulk mild or spicy Italian sausage

1 teaspoon kosher salt

½ teaspoon freshly ground black pepper

One 24-ounce jar arrabbiata or marinara sauce

⅓ cup plus ¼ cup store-bought basil pesto or Lemon Basil Pesto (page 8)

Grated zest of ½ lemon

6 ounces no-boil oven-ready lasagna noodles (sub gluten-free no-boil lasagna for gluten-free)

½ pound fresh mozzarella cheese, thinly sliced

Fresh basil leaves, for serving

*I like to call this my "lazy girl lasagna." While my Italian grandfather would gasp at the thought of this one-skillet wonder, I know if he were still alive, he'd take one bite and then quickly devour the entire pan. Inspired by my love for lasagna, one-pot meals, and the Lasagna Hamburger Helper, this recipe is the ultimate way to feed my hungry family with very little effort. Feel free to swap in regular marinara instead of the arrabbiata sauce if you are sensitive to heat; however, we don't find this dish spicy at all—the arrabbiata just kicks the flavor up a notch!*

PREHEAT the oven to 375°F.

IN a 10-inch ovenproof skillet (preferably cast-iron), heat the oil over medium-high heat. Add the onion and garlic and cook, stirring, until the onion is tender, about 3 minutes. Add the ground beef and sausage. Continue to cook, breaking up the meat with the edge of a spoon, until it is browned and cooked through, 5 to 6 minutes.

DRAIN off the excess fat, then add the salt, pepper, arrabbiata sauce, ⅓ cup of the pesto, and the lemon zest and stir to combine. Bring to a simmer and reduce the heat to medium-low.

CAREFULLY break up the lasagna noodles into 1- to 2-inch pieces and add them to the skillet. Don't worry if they get a little jagged and imperfect, it will still come together nicely. Gently fold the noodles into the sauce to ensure they are coated in the sauce, then use the back of a spatula to spread the contents of the skillet into an even layer.

PLACE the mozzarella slices evenly across the top of the skillet in a single layer, then dollop small spoonfuls of the remaining ¼ cup pesto across the top. Carefully cover the skillet with aluminum foil, ensuring the foil does not touch the top of the lasagna.

BAKE for 15 minutes. Carefully remove the foil and continue to bake, uncovered, until the cheese is golden, 10 to 12 more minutes.

REMOVE the lasagna from the oven and let cool, uncovered, for 8 to 10 minutes to allow the sauce to settle and thicken a bit more. Top with the basil and serve.

# creamy goat cheese pasta with spinach and artichokes

VEGETARIAN

*if modified:*
GLUTEN-FREE

**MAKES 4 SERVINGS** • **TOTAL TIME: 25 MINUTES**

Kosher salt

12 ounces cavatappi or fusilli (sub gluten-free pasta for gluten-free)

2 tablespoons extra-virgin olive oil

½ cup halved and thinly sliced shallot (about 1 large shallot)

2 garlic cloves, minced

½ teaspoon crushed red pepper flakes, plus more for serving (optional)

½ cup dry white wine

6 ounces goat cheese (see note)

Grated zest of ½ lemon

2 tablespoons freshly squeezed lemon juice (about 1 lemon)

½ teaspoon freshly ground black pepper

8 cups packed baby spinach, roughly chopped

One 14-ounce can quartered artichoke hearts, drained and roughly chopped

2 tablespoons finely chopped fresh chives

*This super-simple pasta dinner comes together in less than 30 minutes and is exceptionally tasty. The secret is the tangy, creamy goat cheese, which instantly melts and makes the most amazing sauce. With the classic combination of spinach and artichokes, this recipe is excellent as is, but is also great topped with grilled chicken or shrimp for added protein.*

BRING a large pot of water to a boil. Add a heavy pinch of salt (about 1 tablespoon) and the pasta to the boiling water and cook to al dente according to the package directions.

RESERVING ½ cup of the starchy pasta water, drain the pasta and set aside.

IN a large deep skillet, heat the oil over medium heat. Add the shallot, garlic, and pepper flakes and sauté, stirring, until the shallot is just tender, about 2 minutes. Add the wine to the skillet and cook, stirring, until the wine has reduced by half, about 2 minutes.

ADD the goat cheese, ¼ cup reserved pasta water, the lemon zest, lemon juice, 1 teaspoon kosher salt, and the black pepper. Stir until the cheese has melted and the sauce is smooth.

ADD the spinach and artichoke hearts and cook, stirring, until the spinach just begins to wilt and is combined with the sauce, about 3 minutes. Add the drained pasta to the skillet and constantly toss until the sauce has coated the pasta and the spinach is evenly distributed. Add the remaining ¼ cup pasta water if the sauce seems too thick. Continue stirring until the pasta is well coated and glossy.

DIVIDE among four bowls and top with the chives and additional pepper flakes (if using).

## FROM MY KITCHEN TO YOURS

It is important to use a log of goat cheese instead of the precrumbled. The log melts much better!

# one-pot green curry veggie noodles

**MAKES 2 SERVINGS** • **TOTAL TIME: 25 MINUTES**

2 tablespoons avocado oil

1 cup halved and thinly sliced yellow onion (about 1 small onion)

2 cups stemmed and sliced shiitake mushrooms

½ teaspoon kosher salt, plus more to taste

¼ teaspoon freshly ground black pepper

4 cups roughly chopped bok choy (about 1 large head)

1½ tablespoons Thai green curry paste (see note; I use Mae Ploy brand)

1 cup low-sodium vegetable broth

1 cup unsweetened full-fat coconut milk

2 packages ramen noodles, minus the seasoning packets

1 tablespoon freshly squeezed lime juice (about ½ lime)

¼ cup chopped fresh cilantro leaves

2 tablespoons thinly sliced fresh Thai basil leaves

FOR SERVING

¼ cup roughly chopped unsalted roasted peanuts

2 green onions, thinly sliced on the diagonal

Chopped fresh cilantro

Sliced fresh Thai basil leaves

Lime wedges

*If you're feeling tired at the end of the day and want a cozy, super-simple, and extremely flavorful dish—this is it. This one-pot pasta will quickly become a go-to for busy weeknights. Simply sauté up the veggies, stir in some store-bought Thai green curry paste, broth, and coconut milk and nestle two packages of ramen noodles right into the sauce. You'll have dinner on the table in no time!*

IN a large deep skillet, heat the oil over medium heat. Add the onion, mushrooms, salt, and pepper. Sauté, stirring, until the onion begins to soften, about 3 minutes. Add the bok choy and sauté for another 2 minutes, until it turns bright green and just begins to soften.

ADD the green curry paste to the vegetable mixture and toss to combine with the vegetables. Toast the curry until it is fragrant, about 1 minute.

WHILE stirring, add the broth and coconut milk. Bring to a simmer, then reduce the heat to medium and nestle in the ramen noodles. Cook the ramen for 2 minutes undisturbed. Flip the noodles over and cook for another 2 minutes, undisturbed. Continue cooking the noodles, tossing, until the sauce is thickened and the noodles are tender and well coated, about 2 more minutes. Remove from the heat.

ADD the lime juice, cilantro, and Thai basil and toss to combine.

TO SERVE: Divide between two bowls and top with the peanuts, green onions, cilantro, and Thai basil. Serve with lime wedges.

## FROM MY KITCHEN TO YOURS

When it comes to store-bought curry pastes, green curry typically packs the most heat and some brands can be much spicier than others. This recipe definitely tends toward the spicier side, so if you are sensitive to heat, I recommend adjusting the green curry paste to 1 tablespoon. This recipe also works great with red curry paste, which is a bit milder!

# sun-dried tomato, pesto, and mint pasta

**MAKES 4 SERVINGS** • **TOTAL TIME: 25 MINUTES**

Kosher salt

12 ounces fusilli col buco (sub brown rice linguine for gluten-free)

One 7-ounce jar sun-dried tomatoes in olive oil, thinly sliced, oil reserved

¼ cup minced shallot (about 1 large shallot)

½ teaspoon crushed red pepper flakes, plus more for serving

2 garlic cloves, minced

1 large zucchini, julienned (see note)

½ teaspoon freshly ground black pepper, plus more to taste

1 cup store-bought basil pesto or Lemon Basil Pesto (page 8)

¼ cup roughly chopped fresh mint leaves, plus more for serving

2 tablespoons freshly squeezed lemon juice (about 1 lemon)

Grated parmesan cheese, for serving (omit for dairy-free)

### FROM MY KITCHEN TO YOURS

To julienne the zucchini, cut off the ends, then cut the zucchini lengthwise into ¼-inch-thick slices. You should be able to cut 3 to 4 planks. One plank at a time, cut crosswise on the diagonal into ¼-inch-wide strips.

*Trying to decide what to prepare for dinner can be stressful. On nights when I'm feeling overwhelmed with making that decision, pasta is typically the answer. In this recipe, whether you make your own pesto or buy your favorite store-bought pesto, it turns out delicious every time. It's herbaceous already thanks to the basil pesto, but the addition of mint bumps up the flavor a notch and the sun-dried tomatoes add the perfect sweet yet tart bite.*

BRING a large pot of water to a boil. Add a heavy pinch of salt (about 1 tablespoon) and the pasta to the boiling water and cook al dente according to the package directions.

MEANWHILE, in a large deep skillet, heat 2 tablespoons of the oil from the sun-dried tomatoes over medium heat. Add the shallot, pepper flakes, garlic, zucchini, ½ teaspoon salt, and the black pepper and sauté until the zucchini is tender and slightly golden, 4 to 5 minutes. Add the sun-dried tomatoes and sauté for another 2 minutes.

WHEN the pasta has finished cooking, reserve about 1 cup of the starchy pasta water and set it aside. Drain the pasta and transfer it to the skillet with the zucchini mixture. Add the pesto. Toss thoroughly for 2 to 3 minutes to allow the sauce to coat the pasta. Add ¼ cup pasta water and toss to combine until the pasta is well coated and glossy.

REMOVE from the heat. Add the mint and lemon juice and toss once more. If the pasta is sticking together or still a bit dry, slowly add increments of pasta water ¼ cup at a time. Season with additional salt and black pepper to taste.

DIVIDE among four bowls and garnish with parmesan cheese (if using), additional pepper flakes, and mint.

# creamy dijon penne with kielbasa

**MAKES 4 SERVINGS • TOTAL TIME: 25 MINUTES**

Kosher salt

8 ounces gluten-free penne or rigatoni pasta

2 tablespoons extra-virgin olive oil, divided

One 14-ounce kielbasa sausage, halved lengthwise and thinly sliced crosswise

4 garlic cloves, minced

½ cup minced shallot (about 2 large shallots)

½ teaspoon crushed red pepper flakes

½ cup dry white wine

3 tablespoons Dijon mustard

½ cup unsweetened full-fat coconut milk

1 tablespoon roughly chopped fresh tarragon

½ teaspoon freshly ground black pepper

3 cups baby kale

*In my college years, one of my go-to meals to make was kielbasa pasta. While this recipe is a much more elevated version of the one from my college days, it still gives me all the cozy-yet-simple vibes. Shallot and garlic are sautéed until fragrant, then simmered in a creamy Dijon sauce that is infused with a lovely touch of tarragon and a splash of white wine. I am in love with this easy pasta dish!*

BRING a large pot of water to a boil. Add plenty of salt (about 1 tablespoon) and the pasta and cook to al dente according to the package directions.

MEANWHILE, in a large deep skillet, heat 1 tablespoon of the oil over medium heat. Add the kielbasa and spread it into a single layer. Cook, undisturbed, until browned on one side, about 2 minutes. Toss and continue to cook for 1 to 2 more minutes to finish cooking through. Using a slotted spoon, remove the kielbasa to a plate and set aside.

REDUCE the heat under the skillet to medium-low. Add the remaining 1 tablespoon oil, the garlic, shallot, ½ teaspoon salt, and the pepper flakes and cook, stirring, until the shallot has softened, about 2 minutes.

ADD the wine and cook, stirring, until the wine has reduced by half, 1 to 2 minutes. Add the mustard and whisk until it has emulsified in the sauce. Add the coconut milk, tarragon, ½ teaspoon salt, and the black pepper and whisk until smooth.

RESERVE 1 cup of the starchy pasta water and drain the pasta. Increase the heat under the skillet to medium and add the drained pasta and the kielbasa (and any juices from the plate) and toss to coat. Stir in ¼ cup of the reserved pasta water. Add the baby kale 1 cup at a time and toss until the kale is wilted and well distributed. If needed, add more pasta water, ¼ cup at a time, to bring the sauce together until the pasta is well coated and glossy.

# beef and broccoli lo mein

MAKES 4 SERVINGS  •  TOTAL TIME: 40 MINUTES

### FOR THE SAUCE

4 garlic cloves, minced

1-inch piece fresh ginger, peeled and finely grated

⅔ cup coconut aminos

2 tablespoons coconut sugar

2 tablespoons rice vinegar

2 tablespoons freshly squeezed lime juice (about 1 lime)

2 teaspoons toasted sesame oil

1 teaspoon fish sauce (I use Red Boat brand)

½ teaspoon crushed red pepper flakes

### FOR THE BEEF

1 pound flap or sirloin steak, thinly sliced against the grain

1 teaspoon kosher salt

½ teaspoon freshly ground black pepper

2 tablespoons tapioca flour

1 tablespoon avocado oil

### FOR THE NOODLES

Kosher salt

8 ounces dried lo mein, chow mein, or ramen noodles (sub brown rice linguine for gluten-free)

### FOR FINISHING

2 tablespoons avocado oil, plus more as needed

1 broccoli head, cut into small florets (about 3 cups)

4 green onions, thinly sliced on the diagonal

2 tablespoons toasted sesame seeds, for serving

*Beef and Broccoli is a takeout classic for a reason—it's mild in spice, savory, and dependable! Here's a recipe for a healthier lo mein that is quick to make and an absolute crowd-pleaser. The chewy noodles and tender beef make for a weeknight dinner that will leave your family satisfied and, bonus, you can add as many vegetables as you'd like, making this an all-in-one meal with no sides needed. I use broccoli here, but bell peppers, carrots, and snow peas would be delicious additions!*

BRING a large pot of water to a boil for the noodles.

MAKE THE SAUCE: In a small bowl, whisk together the sauce ingredients. Set aside.

MEANWHILE, PREPARE THE BEEF: In a large bowl, combine the sliced steak, salt, black pepper, tapioca flour, and avocado oil. Toss until the steak is evenly coated. Set aside.

COOK THE NOODLES: When the water is boiling, add plenty of salt (about 1 tablespoon) and the noodles. Cook until tender, about 3 minutes or according to the package directions. Reserve ½ cup of the starchy pasta water, drain the noodles, and rinse under cold water. Set aside.

TO FINISH: In a large deep skillet, heat the avocado oil over medium-high heat. Add the steak in a single layer and cook until golden brown on all sides and cooked through, 2 to 3 minutes per side. Transfer to a clean plate and set aside.

TO the same skillet, add the broccoli florets (if the skillet seems dry, add another tablespoon of avocado oil) and cook, tossing, until slightly tender, 2 to 3 minutes. Add ¼ cup reserved pasta water and partially steam the broccoli, uncovered, until it turns bright green and the liquid has evaporated, about 2 more minutes.

REDUCE the heat to medium and add the green onions, drained noodles, beef, and any of its juices to the skillet. Toss to combine. Pour in the sauce and the remaining reserved pasta water and toss constantly until the noodles are coated and the sauce has started to thicken, about 2 more minutes.

DIVIDE among four bowls and top with toasted sesame seeds.

# calabrian chile pasta pomodoro

**MAKES 4 SERVINGS** • **TOTAL TIME: 20 MINUTES**

Kosher salt

8 ounces bucatini (sub brown rice linguine for gluten-free)

2 tablespoons extra-virgin olive oil

4 garlic cloves, minced

2 pints grape tomatoes

1 tablespoon Calabrian chiles (see note)

½ teaspoon freshly ground black pepper, plus more to taste

½ cup torn fresh basil leaves, plus more for serving

## FROM MY KITCHEN TO YOURS

Calabrian chiles are spicy, smoky peppers from Southern Italy. They are incredibly versatile and pack just the right amount of heat without being overpowering. One of the most common ways to buy Calabrian chiles is the crushed style, where they are ground into a paste along with oil, vinegar, and salt. The resulting chile paste resembles sambal. You can find it in most grocery stores in the condiment section or near the pickles and olives. If you're sensitive to heat, I'd recommend using just 1 teaspoon of the Calabrian chiles in this recipe.

*Pasta pomodoro is one of those simple pleasures in life. Pasta, olive oil, garlic, tomatoes, and basil come together for a simple dish that just never gets old. I fell in love with it on my first trip to Italy and love to make it at home when I don't feel like cooking but still want something delicious. As a spice lover, I use Calabrian chiles in my pasta pomodoro for an extra kick. They add a lovely touch of salt, tang, and, of course, spice, to any dish!*

BRING a large pot of water to a boil. Add plenty of salt (about 1 tablespoon) and the pasta to the boiling water and cook to al dente according to the package directions.

MEANWHILE, in a large deep skillet, heat the oil over medium heat. Add the garlic, tomatoes, Calabrian chiles, 1 teaspoon salt, and the black pepper. Sauté, stirring, until the tomatoes begin to burst, about 6 minutes.

WITH the sauce still lightly simmering, using a potato masher or the back of a fork, gently press the tomatoes to completely burst and release their juices. Stir to combine. Reduce the heat to low while the pasta finishes cooking.

RESERVING 1 cup of the starchy pasta water, drain the pasta. Add the drained pasta to the sauce and increase the heat to medium. Constantly toss the pasta to coat it in the tomatoes, adding the reserved pasta water ¼ cup at a time until the pasta is coated in the sauce and glossy. You likely will not need all the pasta water; I usually end up using ½ to ¾ cup. Remove it from the heat.

ADD the basil and toss to combine. Taste and adjust the seasoning as desired.

DIVIDE among four bowls and top with some torn basil leaves.

# tarragon mushroom orzo-tto

**MAKES 4 TO 6 SERVINGS** • **TOTAL TIME: 35 MINUTES**

VEGETARIAN

*if modified:*
GLUTEN-FREE

4 tablespoons extra-virgin olive oil, divided

½ cup finely diced yellow onion (about ½ small onion)

6 cups thinly sliced mixed mushrooms (see note)

2 teaspoons kosher salt, divided

½ teaspoon freshly ground black pepper, plus more for serving

2 garlic cloves, minced

2 cups orzo pasta (sub gluten-free orzo for gluten-free)

¾ cup dry white wine

3 cups low-sodium vegetable broth

3 tablespoons finely chopped fresh tarragon leaves, divided, plus more for serving

Grated zest of ½ lemon

2 tablespoons freshly squeezed lemon juice (about 1 lemon)

½ cup freshly grated parmesan cheese, plus more for serving

*What we all love about a traditional risotto is captured here by our lovable friend orzo. Making this "risotto" with orzo pasta is a great alternative to the more traditional Italian rice risotto. Although it isn't quite as creamy, it's still decadent and a lot quicker to make. An array of meaty mushrooms and herbaceous tarragon makes this meal feel restaurant worthy for any weeknight!*

IN a large pot or Dutch oven, heat 2 tablespoons of the oil over medium-high heat. Add the onion and cook, stirring, until the onion is tender, 1 to 2 minutes.

ADD the mushrooms, 1 teaspoon of the salt, and the pepper and toss to combine. Cook, tossing occasionally, until the mushrooms are tender and lightly golden, about 5 minutes. Add the garlic and stir, sautéing for 2 minutes more. Transfer the mushroom mixture to a large bowl. Set aside.

ADD the remaining 2 tablespoons oil to the pot. Add the orzo and the remaining 1 teaspoon salt and cook, stirring often, until the orzo is toasted, about 1 minute. Add the wine and continue to cook, stirring and scraping up any browned bits from the bottom of the pot, until the wine is just absorbed, about 1 minute.

STIR in the broth, 2 tablespoons of the tarragon, and the lemon zest and bring to a boil. Reduce the heat to a simmer and cook, stirring often, until the orzo is tender and has absorbed the liquid, 10 to 12 minutes.

REMOVE from the heat and add the remaining 1 tablespoon tarragon, the lemon juice, mushroom mixture, and parmesan. Gently fold to combine. Taste and adjust the seasoning if needed.

SERVE topped with some additional parmesan and freshly ground black pepper.

## FROM MY KITCHEN TO YOURS

I usually use a combination of at least two types of mushrooms. My favorites in this dish are shiitake, baby bella, and trumpet.

98     ONE-PAN COCONUT-LIME CHICKEN AND RICE

101     SKILLET CHICKEN CACCIATORE

102     CRISPY BUFFALO CHICKEN LETTUCE WRAPS WITH BLUE CHEESE SAUCE

104     CURRY CHICKEN SKILLET WITH SWEET POTATOES

107     SOUR CREAM CHICKEN ENCHILADAS

108     SAUCY GOCHUJANG CHICKEN STIR-FRY

111     SKILLET BBQ CHICKEN QUINOA BAKE

112     CHIPOTLE TURKEY–STUFFED POBLANO PEPPERS

115     SHEET PAN HOT HONEY DIJON CHICKEN

116     SLOW COOKER OR PRESSURE COOKER BEER-BRAISED CHICKEN TACOS

118     CASHEW CHICKEN STIR-FRY

121     SLOW COOKER OR PRESSURE COOKER CREAMY ENCHILADA CHICKEN

122     SKILLET CHICKEN AND VEGGIES WITH "PEANUT" SAUCE

125     JERK-INSPIRED CHICKEN TACOS

126     CHICKEN PICCATA MEATBALLS

129     GREEK-INSPIRED CHICKEN AND ORZO BAKE

130     GINGER AND PEANUT BUTTER GROUND TURKEY STIR-FRY

poultry

# one-pan coconut-lime chicken and rice

**MAKES 4 SERVINGS • TOTAL TIME: 1 HOUR**

## FOR THE CHICKEN

2 pounds bone-in, skin-on chicken thighs, trimmed of excess fat

1 teaspoon kosher salt

½ teaspoon freshly ground black pepper

Grated zest of ½ lime

2 tablespoons avocado oil

## FOR THE RICE

½ cup thinly sliced shallot (about 1 large shallot)

3 garlic cloves, minced

1-inch piece fresh ginger, peeled and finely grated

1 to 3 Thai chiles or serrano peppers, very thinly sliced (1 for mild, 3 for hot)

1 cup white jasmine rice, rinsed well and drained

4 green onions, thinly sliced on the diagonal, white and green parts kept separate

¼ teaspoon kosher salt

Grated zest of ½ lime

2 tablespoons freshly squeezed lime juice (about 1 lime)

1 tablespoon fish sauce (I use Red Boat brand)

¼ cup loosely chopped fresh cilantro leaves and tender stems

1 cup unsweetened full-fat coconut milk

½ cup low-sodium chicken broth

## FOR SERVING

¼ cup fresh cilantro leaves

1 lime, cut into wedges

*Are you on the fence about chicken thighs? First off, I do not know why you would be, but regardless, I am pretty confident that this recipe will change your mind. This roasted chicken over fluffy rice is an absolutely wonderful twist on a classic weeknight staple. Enhanced by Thai-inspired ingredients like coconut milk, fish sauce, garlic, ginger, and Thai chiles—it's the perfect one-pot umami-packed skillet. This dreamy dinner is one you'll want to keep making forever and ever.*

**PREHEAT** the oven to 350°F.

**BROWN THE CHICKEN:** Pat the chicken dry with a paper towel. In a small bowl, combine the salt, black pepper, and lime zest. Rub the mixture into the skin side of the chicken thighs, really pressing the seasoning in so the lime zest sticks.

**IN** a large deep ovenproof skillet with a fitted lid, heat the oil over medium heat. Add the chicken skin side down in a single layer and cook undisturbed until golden brown and crispy, 6 to 7 minutes. The chicken will not be fully cooked through as it will continue to cook in the oven. Transfer to a plate and set aside.

**PREPARE THE RICE:** In the same skillet, reduce the heat to medium-low. Discard all but 2 tablespoons of fat from the pan. Add the shallot, garlic, ginger, and chiles and sauté until tender, about 1 minute. Add the rice, the white parts of the green onion, and the salt. Cook, stirring, toasting the rice until fragrant and lightly browned, 2 to 3 minutes.

**STIR** in the lime zest, lime juice, fish sauce, cilantro, coconut milk, and chicken broth. Bring to a simmer. Nestle the chicken thighs back into the skillet, skin side up.

**COVER** the skillet, carefully transfer to the oven, and bake for 25 minutes. Carefully uncover the skillet and continue baking until the rice is tender, the chicken is cooked through, and the skin is crisp, 10 more minutes.

**REMOVE** from the oven, fluff the rice with a fork, and let rest for 5 minutes.

**TO SERVE:** Garnish with the green parts of the green onion and the cilantro leaves. Serve with fresh lime wedges.

# skillet chicken cacciatore

**MAKES 4 SERVINGS • TOTAL TIME: 45 MINUTES**

4 boneless, skinless chicken breasts

1¼ teaspoons kosher salt, divided

½ teaspoon freshly ground black pepper

3 tablespoons cassava flour

2 tablespoons extra-virgin olive oil

3 ounces diced pancetta

½ cup halved and thinly sliced shallot (about 1 large shallot)

½ cup finely diced celery (about 1 stalk)

2 garlic cloves, minced

½ teaspoon dried oregano

2 cups sliced baby bella mushrooms

1 tablespoon tomato paste

½ teaspoon crushed red pepper flakes

¾ cup dry white wine

One 14.5-ounce can crushed tomatoes

2 tablespoons capers, drained and rinsed

1 fresh rosemary sprig

2 tablespoons finely chopped fresh parsley

*Hearty and satisfying, chicken cacciatore is a rustic Italian classic. Chicken is cooked until tender in a rich tomato sauce with white wine, mushrooms, capers, and rosemary. The dish is so savory and wholesome, but the best part? It is made entirely in one skillet, making this Italian comfort meal come together quickly enough for weeknights. It's delicious with roasted vegetables, a big salad, or a side of pasta, if you'd like!*

PLACE the chicken breasts on a cutting board and cover with parchment paper or plastic wrap. Using a meat mallet or the bottom of a heavy skillet, pound the chicken to a uniform ½-inch thickness. Pat dry with paper towels and season both sides of the chicken evenly with 1 teaspoon of the salt and the black pepper.

PLACE the cassava flour in a shallow bowl. Dredge each piece of chicken in the flour until well coated on both sides, shaking off any excess.

IN a large skillet, heat the oil over medium-high heat until shimmering. Place the chicken in the skillet, working in batches as needed, and cook until golden brown on both sides, about 3 minutes per side. The chicken doesn't need to be fully cooked through as it will continue to cook in the sauce. Transfer the browned chicken to a clean plate and set aside.

ADD the pancetta to the skillet and cook, stirring occasionally, until the fat renders and the pancetta begins to crisp, about 4 minutes. Reduce the heat to medium and add the shallot, celery, garlic, and oregano. Continue to cook, stirring, until the veggies are tender, about 2 more minutes.

ADD the mushrooms, tomato paste, pepper flakes, and the remaining ¼ teaspoon salt. Toss to combine, ensuring that the tomato paste gets evenly distributed. Pour in the wine and cook, stirring, until the wine has reduced by about half and the mushrooms are tender, about 4 minutes.

ADD the tomatoes and capers, stir to combine, and bring to a simmer. Reduce the heat to a light simmer and nestle the chicken and any of its juices back into the skillet. Add the rosemary sprig, cover, and cook until the chicken is cooked through, 9 to 11 minutes.

REMOVE from the heat and discard the rosemary. Serve garnished with the parsley.

# crispy buffalo chicken lettuce wraps with blue cheese sauce

**MAKES 4 SERVINGS** • **TOTAL TIME: 35 MINUTES**

## FOR THE BLUE CHEESE SAUCE

½ cup plain 2% or whole-milk Greek yogurt

½ cup blue cheese crumbles, divided

1 teaspoon grated lemon zest

2 tablespoons freshly squeezed lemon juice (about 1 lemon)

1 teaspoon apple cider vinegar

¼ teaspoon kosher salt

½ teaspoon freshly ground black pepper

1 tablespoon chopped fresh chives

## FOR THE CRUNCHY BUFFALO CHICKEN

1 large egg

¾ cup gluten-free panko bread crumbs (I use Aleia's brand)

3 tablespoons cassava flour

1 pound boneless, skinless chicken tenders

½ teaspoon kosher salt

½ teaspoon freshly ground black pepper

2 tablespoons avocado oil, plus more as needed

½ cup Buffalo hot sauce (I use Frank's brand)

## FOR SERVING

1 large head iceberg lettuce, separated into leaves (see note)

½ cup matchstick-cut carrots (about ¼ medium carrot)

½ cup roughly chopped fresh dill fronds

*When busy weeknights begin to take over, there is nothing quite like turning to a bottle of Buffalo sauce to help save the day. The tangy, spicy sauce can add a bold kick of flavor to grilled chicken, burgers, and salads in minutes. I love making these panko-breaded chicken tenders, tossing them in Buffalo sauce, and serving them in lettuce wraps with a simple blue cheese sauce. It's like a little salad you can eat with your hands—one of my favorite go-to meals!*

**MAKE THE BLUE CHEESE SAUCE:** In a blender or using an immersion blender in a wide-mouth jar, combine the yogurt, ¼ cup of the blue cheese crumbles, the lemon zest, lemon juice, vinegar, salt, and pepper. Blend until smooth. Stir in the remaining ¼ cup blue cheese crumbles and the chives. Set aside in the fridge until serving. This keeps well in the fridge for up to 5 days.

**MAKE THE CRUNCHY BUFFALO CHICKEN:** In a shallow bowl, whisk together the egg and 1 tablespoon water. In a second shallow bowl, combine the panko and cassava flour and stir until well combined. Set the bowls next to each other for dredging.

**PAT** the chicken dry with a paper towel and season both sides of each piece with the salt and pepper. Dip a piece of chicken first in the egg mixture and shake off the excess. Then dredge the chicken in the panko mixture, pressing the mixture into the chicken to help it adhere. Set aside. Repeat with the remaining pieces of chicken.

**LINE** a large plate with paper towels. In a large deep nonstick skillet, heat the oil over medium heat until it is shimmering. Working in batches, carefully lay the chicken into the oil in a single layer. Fry until golden brown on both sides and cooked through, 3 to 5 minutes per side

**TRANSFER** the cooked chicken to the plate lined with paper towels. Use a paper towel to carefully wipe down the skillet to remove any burned bits in between batches. If the skillet runs dry as you're cooking the chicken, add more oil as needed.

**WHEN** all the chicken is cooked, return it to the skillet and pour in the Buffalo sauce. Using a silicone spatula, gently toss the chicken in the sauce to combine.

**TO SERVE:** Remove the chicken from the skillet and add to a serving platter along with the lettuce leaves, carrots, and dill. To eat, layer two lettuce leaves and place the carrots in the bottom. Add a chicken tender, top with a dollop of the blue cheese sauce, and garnish with dill.

## FROM MY KITCHEN TO YOURS

To prepare the iceberg lettuce for wraps, first peel off the outer layer that feels soft and flimsy (usually the first layer or two are not very crisp). Next, cut the head in half down the center (keeping the core intact). Begin to carefully peel the outer layers of lettuce to use for wraps. As you work your way down the lettuce leaves, it may be easier to peel the leaves off two at a time. Trim any pieces of core from the lettuce leaves. For sturdier wraps, layer two lettuce leaves atop one another.

# curry chicken skillet with sweet potatoes

**MAKES 4 SERVINGS** • **TOTAL TIME: 50 MINUTES**

4 small boneless, skinless chicken breasts

1½ teaspoons kosher salt, divided

1 teaspoon freshly ground black pepper, divided

3 tablespoons cassava flour

2 tablespoons extra-virgin olive oil

2 garlic cloves, minced

1-inch piece fresh ginger, peeled and finely grated

¾ cup small-diced yellow onion (about ½ medium onion)

1 red bell pepper, sliced into ¼-inch-wide strips

2 cups peeled and ½-inch cubed sweet potato (about 1 large potato)

1 tablespoon yellow curry powder

1 teaspoon ground cumin

1 teaspoon ground turmeric

¼ teaspoon cayenne pepper

2 tablespoons tomato paste

½ cup low-sodium chicken broth

1 cup unsweetened full-fat coconut milk

4 cups baby spinach

1 tablespoon freshly squeezed lime juice (about ½ lime)

2 tablespoons roughly chopped fresh cilantro leaves, optional

*Chicken and potatoes is a classic weeknight combination. Here, I've turned things up a notch. Filled with warm and bold flavors like curry powder, ginger, and cumin, it's the perfect cozy dish. My favorite thing about it is that it has everything that you need in one skillet—your sweet potatoes, veggies, and chicken for a complete, filling dish.*

PLACE the chicken on a cutting board and cover with parchment paper or plastic wrap. Using a meat mallet or the bottom of a heavy skillet, pound the chicken to a uniform ½-inch thickness. Pat dry with paper towels. Season both sides of the chicken evenly with 1 teaspoon of the salt and ½ teaspoon of the black pepper.

PLACE the cassava flour in a large shallow bowl. Dredge the chicken in the flour, pressing it in to help it adhere.

IN a large deep skillet, heat the oil over medium heat. Carefully lay the chicken in the oil and fry until golden brown on both sides, about 3 minutes per side. The chicken does not need to be cooked through as it will finish cooking in the sauce. Transfer the chicken to a clean plate and set aside.

REDUCE the heat under the skillet to medium. Add the garlic, ginger, onion, bell pepper, sweet potato, and remaining ½ teaspoon salt and ½ teaspoon black pepper. Cook, stirring, until the onions are tender, about 3 minutes.

ADD the curry powder, cumin, turmeric, and cayenne and cook, stirring, until the spices are toasted and fragrant, about 1 minute. Add the tomato paste and stir until well incorporated with the veggies. Slowly pour the broth into the skillet, continuing to stir until it is well incorporated and the tomato paste is smooth. Repeat with the coconut milk, ensuring it's well combined. Bring to a simmer. Once bubbling, reduce the heat to medium-low so that the sauce is just lightly simmering.

ADD the spinach to the skillet and fold it into the sauce until just wilted, about 1 minute. Nestle the chicken back into the skillet. Cover and cook until the sweet potatoes are tender and chicken is cooked through, about 10 minutes.

FINISH with the lime juice. If desired, garnish with the cilantro.

# sour cream chicken enchiladas

GLUTEN-FREE

GRAIN-FREE

**MAKES 4 SERVINGS** • **TOTAL TIME: 1 HOUR**

**Softened butter for the baking dish**

**FOR THE SOUR CREAM SAUCE**

2 tablespoons unsalted butter

2 tablespoons tapioca or arrowroot flour

½ teaspoon ground cumin

½ teaspoon kosher salt

⅔ cup low-sodium chicken broth

1 cup salsa verde

⅔ cup sour cream

**FOR THE FILLING**

4 cups shredded cooked chicken (I use a rotisserie chicken)

One 4-ounce can mild diced green chiles

½ cup shredded Monterey Jack cheese

½ teaspoon kosher salt

**FOR THE ENCHILADAS**

8 grain-free tortillas (I use Siete brand)

½ cup shredded Monterey Jack cheese

2 tablespoons salsa verde

½ jalapeño, very thinly sliced, optional

2 tablespoons fresh cilantro leaves

¼ cup finely diced red onion (about ¼ small onion)

*When I was growing up, my mom used to make sour cream chicken enchiladas on busy weeknights. I've adapted her recipe in my own kitchen, and while it has updated ingredients, it still comes together very easily! The sour cream sauce is a force to be reckoned with.*

PREHEAT the oven to 375°F. Grease a 9 × 13-inch baking dish with butter.

MAKE THE SOUR CREAM SAUCE: In a small saucepan, melt the butter over medium heat. Add the tapioca flour and whisk until just combined. Add the cumin and salt and whisk to combine. Toast the cumin for about 2 minutes, stirring constantly and taking care that it doesn't burn.

SLOWLY add the chicken broth, whisking constantly until well incorporated with the tapioca mixture, then continue to whisk while you pour in the salsa verde. Cook, still whisking constantly, until the sauce thickens, 1 to 2 minutes.

REMOVE from the heat and whisk in the sour cream until smooth. Set aside. The sauce might feel overly thick, but don't worry—as it cooks, the consistency works perfectly.

MAKE THE FILLING: In a large bowl, combine the shredded chicken, ½ cup of the sour cream sauce, the diced green chiles, Monterey Jack, and salt. Stir until well combined. Set aside.

ASSEMBLE THE ENCHILADAS: Spread ½ cup of the sour cream sauce in the prepared baking dish to evenly coat the bottom.

ONE at a time, place the tortillas in a dry (no oil) stainless steel skillet over medium heat and warm them for about 30 seconds on each side to make them more pliable. Fill each warmed tortilla with about ⅓ cup of the filling, gently roll them up, and place them seam side down in the baking dish.

POUR the remaining sour cream sauce evenly over the enchiladas. Top with the Monterey Jack, the salsa verde, and the jalapeño slices (if using).

BAKE, uncovered, until the cheese is melted and the sauce is bubbling, about 20 minutes. Turn the oven to broil and cook, watching carefully so as not to burn, until the cheese is golden and bubbling, 2 to 4 minutes.

SET aside to cool for 5 minutes. Top with the cilantro and red onion and serve.

# saucy gochujang chicken stir-fry

**MAKES 4 SERVINGS** • **TOTAL TIME: 30 MINUTES**

### FOR THE GOCHUJANG SAUCE

2 tablespoons gochujang (I use Mother In Law's brand; sub a gluten-free brand for gluten-free, see page 6)

1 tablespoon unsweetened ketchup

1 tablespoon coconut sugar

1 tablespoon rice vinegar

½ teaspoon toasted sesame oil

¼ cup coconut aminos

¼ cup low-sodium chicken broth

2 garlic cloves, minced

1-inch piece fresh ginger, peeled and grated

½ teaspoon crushed red pepper flakes, optional

### FOR THE STIR-FRY

1½ pounds chicken tenders, cut into 1-inch pieces

3 tablespoons avocado oil, divided, plus more as needed

1 teaspoon kosher salt

½ teaspoon freshly ground black pepper

2 tablespoons tapioca flour

1 pound green beans, trimmed and cut into 1-inch pieces

4 green onions, thinly sliced, plus more for serving

Prepared cauliflower rice or steamed rice, optional for serving

*This simple stir-fry is on permanent rotation in my house. Using a delicious, homemade sauce that leans on one of my favorite condiments, gochujang, it's got an incredible punch of flavor that is a little sweet and a little bit spicy. Depending on what brand you buy, some store-bought gochujang can be spicier than others, so taste your stir-fry before adding red pepper flakes and adjust the heat to your preference.*

**MAKE THE GOCHUJANG SAUCE:** In a medium bowl, combine the sauce ingredients and whisk until smooth. Set aside.

**PREPARE THE STIR-FRY:** In a large bowl, combine the chicken, 1 tablespoon of the avocado oil, the salt, black pepper, and tapioca flour and toss to mix well. Set aside.

**IN** a large deep nonstick skillet, heat the remaining 2 tablespoons of avocado oil over medium-high heat. Working in batches if necessary, so as not to overcrowd the pan, add the chicken in a single layer and sear until a golden-brown crust forms and the chicken is cooked through, 3 to 4 minutes per side. Using a slotted spoon, transfer the chicken to a clean plate and set aside.

**TO** the same skillet, add the green beans and green onion. Cook, tossing occasionally, until the green beans are blistered and tender, about 5 minutes. If the skillet runs dry, add more avocado oil.

**ADD** the reserved sauce and chicken to the skillet. Cook, stirring, until the sauce is thickened and the chicken is well coated, 2 to 3 minutes. Serve as is or over prepared rice. Garnish with additional green onions.

# skillet bbq chicken quinoa bake

MAKES 4 SERVINGS  •  TOTAL TIME: 55 MINUTES

GLUTEN-FREE

*if modified:*
DAIRY-FREE

4 small boneless, skinless chicken breasts

1½ teaspoons kosher salt, divided

¾ teaspoon freshly ground black pepper, divided

3 tablespoons cassava flour

2 tablespoons extra-virgin olive oil, plus more as needed

¾ cup small-diced red onion (about ¾ small onion), divided

¾ cup small-diced red bell pepper

2 garlic cloves, minced

1 cup quinoa

½ teaspoon ground cumin

1 teaspoon dried oregano

½ teaspoon smoked paprika

One 15.5-ounce can black beans, drained and rinsed

1 cup frozen corn kernels

2 cups low-sodium chicken broth

½ cup less-sugar barbecue sauce, divided (I use Noble Made brand)

1 tablespoon freshly squeezed lime juice (about 1 lime)

¼ cup finely chopped fresh cilantro leaves, plus more for garnish

1 cup shredded smoked Gouda cheese (omit for dairy-free)

½ jalapeño, thinly sliced, optional

1 lime, cut into wedges, for serving

*This skillet dinner brings all my favorite flavors from a BBQ chicken pizza into a nutritious quinoa bake. I love the robust flavors of this dish and I especially love that most of the ingredients are pantry staples!*

PREHEAT the oven to 375°F.

PLACE the chicken breasts on a cutting board and cover with parchment paper or plastic wrap and use a meat mallet or the bottom of a heavy skillet to pound the chicken to a uniform ½-inch thickness. Pat dry with a paper towel and season both sides of the chicken evenly with 1 teaspoon of the salt and ½ teaspoon of the black pepper.

POUR the cassava flour into a shallow bowl. One at a time, dredge the chicken pieces in the flour to coat them evenly, shaking off any excess.

IN a cast-iron skillet or other ovenproof skillet, heat the oil over medium-high heat. Working in batches if necessary, so as not to overcrowd the skillet, place the chicken in the skillet and cook until golden brown on each side, 2 to 3 minutes per side. The chicken does not need to be cooked through as it will finish baking in the oven. Transfer the chicken to a plate and set aside.

REDUCE the heat under the skillet to medium and if the skillet seems dry, add another tablespoon of oil. Add ½ cup of the onion, the bell pepper, and garlic and sauté until the onion just begins to soften, about 4 minutes.

ADD the quinoa, cumin, oregano, smoked paprika, and remaining ½ teaspoon salt and ¼ teaspoon black pepper and stir to combine. Cook for about 2 minutes to toast the quinoa and spices.

STIR in the black beans, corn, broth, ¼ cup of the barbecue sauce, the lime juice, and cilantro. Bring to a rapid simmer and nestle the chicken back into the pan.

TRANSFER to the oven and bake, uncovered, for 20 minutes.

REMOVE from the oven and top each chicken breast with 1 tablespoon barbecue sauce. Sprinkle the smoked Gouda (if using) all over the skillet, along with the remaining ¼ cup red onion and the sliced jalapeño (if using). Return to the oven and bake until the cheese is melted and chicken is cooked through, 5 to 8 minutes.

LET rest for 5 minutes, then garnish with some chopped cilantro. Serve with the lime wedges.

# chipotle turkey-stuffed poblano peppers

**MAKES 4 SERVINGS** • **TOTAL TIME: 50 MINUTES**

Nonstick cooking spray

4 medium poblano peppers

2 tablespoons extra-virgin olive oil

¾ cup diced yellow onion (about ½ medium onion)

2 garlic cloves, minced

1 teaspoon kosher salt

½ teaspoon freshly ground black pepper

2 teaspoons smoked paprika

1 teaspoon chipotle chile powder or regular chili powder

1 teaspoon ground cumin

1 teaspoon garlic powder

1 teaspoon dried oregano

1½ pounds ground turkey or chicken, preferably dark meat

2 tablespoons tomato paste

One 4-ounce can mild diced green chiles

One 14.5-ounce can diced fire-roasted tomatoes, drained

1½ cups shredded Monterey Jack cheese, divided

Fresh cilantro leaves, for garnish

*These peppers have it all—they're the perfect blend of meat, cheese, and a delicious smoky chipotle kick to add to your dinner rotation. Chipotle chile powder packs some heat, so if you want less spice, feel free to sub in classic chili seasoning instead.*

PREHEAT the oven to 375°F. Lightly mist a 9 × 13-inch baking dish with cooking spray.

TO soften the poblano peppers before you stuff them, lay the whole peppers in the baking dish and bake for 10 minutes.

MEANWHILE, in a large skillet, heat the oil over medium heat. Add the onion, garlic, salt, and black pepper and sauté until the onion is just tender, about 3 minutes. Add the smoked paprika, chipotle powder, cumin, garlic powder, and oregano. Stir to combine and toast the spices, 1 to 2 minutes.

ADD the turkey to the skillet and cook, breaking it up with the edge of a spoon, until browned and cooked through, 6 to 8 minutes. Add the tomato paste and stir to combine, ensuring the paste is evenly distributed throughout.

ADD the green chiles and canned tomatoes and toss until well combined. Remove from the heat and set aside.

REMOVE the peppers from the oven and leave the oven on. Let the peppers sit until cool enough to handle. Use a paring knife to make a long cut down the center on one side of a pepper and then another perpendicular cut across the top, just under the stem, to make a "T," taking care not to cut all the way through the pepper. You're creating a pocket to add the filling into. Using a spoon, scoop out the seeds and discard. Repeat with each pepper and return them to the baking dish.

ADD 1 tablespoon of the Monterey Jack to the bottom of each pepper. Divide the filling mixture among the peppers until they are very full. Dividing evenly, top the stuffed peppers with the remaining cheese.

COVER the baking dish with foil and bake for 15 minutes. Carefully remove the foil and bake uncovered for 10 more minutes, or until the cheese is bubbling and lightly browned.

TOP with the cilantro and serve.

# sheet pan hot honey dijon chicken

GLUTEN-FREE

DAIRY-FREE

PALEO

GRAIN-FREE

**MAKES 4 SERVINGS • TOTAL TIME: 50 MINUTES**

## FOR THE VEGGIES AND CHICKEN

1 pound baby Dutch yellow potatoes, halved

1 pound Brussels sprouts, trimmed, halved lengthwise

4 ounces diced pancetta

2 Fresno chiles, seeded and thinly sliced

4 tablespoons extra-virgin olive oil, divided

2 teaspoons kosher salt, divided

1 teaspoon freshly ground black pepper, divided

3 pounds bone-in, skin-on chicken thighs, trimmed of excess fat

## FOR THE HOT HONEY DIJON SAUCE

¼ cup extra-virgin olive oil

¼ cup honey

3 tablespoons Dijon mustard

2 tablespoons apple cider vinegar

1 tablespoon freshly squeezed lemon juice (about ½ lemon)

2 teaspoons fresh thyme leaves

½ teaspoon cayenne pepper

¼ teaspoon kosher salt

1 garlic clove, minced

*Sweet and spicy honey Dijon–glazed chicken with Brussels sprouts and potatoes is a perfect weeknight recipe that brings you maximum flavor with minimal ingredients! This dish isn't really that spicy, but if you like your food on the milder side, just omit the cayenne and Fresno chiles, and if you're serving little ones, I'd definitely omit the cayenne.*

PREHEAT the oven to 425°F. Line a sheet pan with parchment paper.

PREPARE THE VEGGIES AND CHICKEN: On the prepared sheet pan, combine the potatoes, Brussels sprouts, pancetta, Fresno chiles, 2 tablespoons of the oil, 1 teaspoon of the salt, and ½ teaspoon of the black pepper. Toss until well coated, then spread the veggies to the edges of the sheet pan, leaving room in the center for the chicken.

LAY the chicken thighs in the center of the sheet pan, skin side up. Pat them dry, then drizzle the skin with the remaining 2 tablespoons oil and season with the remaining 1 teaspoon salt and ½ teaspoon black pepper.

ROAST until the chicken is golden brown, the potatoes are tender, and the edges of the Brussels sprouts are lightly browned and crispy, 30 to 35 minutes.

MEANWHILE, MAKE THE HOT HONEY DIJON SAUCE: In a small bowl, combine the sauce ingredients and whisk until very smooth. Set aside while the chicken and veggies roast.

SPOON 1 tablespoon of the sauce over each chicken thigh and spread so that it evenly coats the tops of the chicken. Drizzle 2 tablespoons of the sauce over the veggies, reserving the rest for serving. Gently toss the veggies to coat evenly. Return to the oven and roast until the sauce is caramelized and the chicken is cooked through, 5 to 8 more minutes, taking care not to let it burn.

REMOVE the sheet pan from the oven and let the chicken and veggies cool for 5 minutes. Serve with the remaining hot honey Dijon sauce for drizzling.

# slow cooker or pressure cooker beer-braised chicken tacos

**MAKES 12 SERVINGS**  •  **TOTAL TIME: 45 MINUTES OR 4 TO 6 HOURS**

## FOR THE CHICKEN

1 tablespoon kosher salt

2 teaspoons smoked paprika

1 teaspoon ground cumin

1 teaspoon garlic powder

1 teaspoon freshly ground black pepper

1½ teaspoons dried oregano

4 pounds boneless, skinless chicken thighs, trimmed of excess fat

2 tablespoons avocado oil, plus more as needed

¼ cup minced canned chipotle peppers in adobo sauce (about 3 peppers)

3 tablespoons tomato paste

Two 4-ounce cans mild diced green chiles

One 12-ounce bottle Modelo Especial, Pacifico, or other light lager

## FOR THE AVOCADO CREMA

1 large avocado, halved and pitted

¼ cup pickled jalapeño slices

2 tablespoons brine from the jalapeño jar

⅓ cup roughly chopped fresh cilantro leaves and tender stems

1 garlic clove, roughly chopped

2 tablespoons freshly squeezed lime juice (about 1 lime)

¼ teaspoon kosher salt

## OPTIONAL FOR SERVING

Corn tortillas or lettuce cups

Shredded iceberg lettuce

Radishes, cut into thin matchsticks

Cilantro leaves

Cotija cheese

Lime wedges

*For these tacos, chicken slowly simmers in a delicious chipotle mixture that is brightened by a bottle of beer—yes, a full bottle. If you've never cooked chicken in beer, you are in for a treat! It adds the perfect flavor to the sauce while also helping to tenderize your chicken. But don't worry, the alcohol cooks off, so this is still wonderful for the whole family. It's a great go-to for busy weeknights with plenty of leftovers, plus fantastic when hosting a football-watching party!*

## FOR BOTH METHODS

**SEASON THE CHICKEN:** In a small bowl, combine the salt, smoked paprika, cumin, garlic powder, black pepper, and oregano. Stir until well incorporated. Season both sides of the chicken with the seasoning mix.

## SLOW COOKER METHOD

IN a large skillet, heat the oil over medium-high heat. When hot, working in batches so as not to overcrowd the skillet, and adding more oil as needed, sear the chicken until golden brown on both sides, 2 to 3 minutes per side, adding more oil to the skillet as needed. The chicken does not need to be cooked through at this stage. Set the chicken aside.

IN a slow cooker, combine the chipotle peppers, tomato paste, green chiles, and beer and whisk until well combined. Nestle the chicken into the sauce, cover, and cook on high for 4 hours or on low for 6 hours.

WHEN the cook time is complete, transfer the chicken to a sheet pan (do not discard the remaining liquid in the slow cooker). Using two forks, shred the chicken, then return it to the slow cooker.

## PRESSURE COOKER METHOD

TURN the pressure cooker on the "sauté" function and heat the oil. When hot, working in batches so as not to overcrowd the pressure cooker, sear the chicken until golden brown on both sides, 2 to 3 minutes per side, adding more oil to the pot as needed. The chicken does not need to be cooked through at this stage. Set the chicken aside.

TO the empty pressure cooker, add the chipotle peppers and tomato paste and stir to toast the paste, about 1 minute. Add the green chiles and beer and stir to combine.

NESTLE the chicken and its juices back into the pressure cooker and hit "cancel." Lock the lid on the pressure cooker and turn the vent to "seal." Press the "manual" or "pressure cook" button (depending on your model) and set the time to 15 minutes. Walk away from the pressure cooker and let it do its thing!

WHEN the cook time is finished, quick-release the pressure. When all the pressure has been released, carefully remove the lid and transfer the chicken to a sheet pan (do not discard the remaining liquid in the pressure cooker). Using two forks, shred the chicken, then return it to the pressure cooker.

## FOR BOTH METHODS

MAKE THE AVOCADO CREMA: In a blender or using an immersion blender in a wide-mouth jar, combine the crema ingredients and blend until smooth.

SERVE the chicken as desired in tortillas or lettuce cups. Top with the avocado crema and any other desired accompaniments.

# cashew chicken stir-fry

**MAKES 4 SERVINGS** • **TOTAL TIME: 45 MINUTES**

## FOR THE SAUCE

⅓ cup low-sodium chicken broth

¼ cup coconut aminos

2 tablespoons rice vinegar

1 tablespoon freshly squeezed lime juice (about ½ lime)

2 tablespoons no-sugar-added sriracha (I use Yellowbird brand), optional

2 tablespoons unsweetened creamy cashew butter

2 tablespoons coconut sugar (omit for Whole30)

1 teaspoon toasted sesame oil

1 teaspoon fish sauce (I use Red Boat brand)

¼ teaspoon Chinese five-spice powder

1-inch piece fresh ginger, peeled and finely grated

4 garlic cloves, minced

## FOR THE CHICKEN

2 pounds boneless, skinless chicken tenders, cut into 1-inch cubes

1 tablespoon avocado oil

1½ teaspoons kosher salt

½ teaspoon freshly ground black pepper

2 tablespoons tapioca flour

## FOR THE STIR-FRY

¾ cup unsalted roasted cashews, plus more for serving

2 tablespoons avocado oil

6 green onions, cut into 1-inch lengths, white and green parts kept separate

Prepared cauliflower rice or steamed rice, optional for serving

1 lime, cut into wedges, for serving

*This dish of stir-fried chicken, roasted cashews, and a savory garlic sauce tastes just like takeout. There's very little chopping for this recipe, and it all comes down to measuring out your ingredients for the delicious sauce. While you can make this spicy by adding sriracha, it's also amazing without the spice! My family loves this recipe, and I usually skip the sriracha for them and add a little touch to my own bowl when serving.*

**MAKE THE SAUCE:** In a medium bowl, whisk together all the sauce ingredients until well combined. Set aside.

**IN** a large bowl, combine the chicken, avocado oil, salt, pepper, and tapioca flour. Toss until well combined. Set aside.

**MAKE THE STIR-FRY:** In a dry (no oil) large nonstick skillet, toast the cashews over medium heat, tossing occasionally, until fragrant, about 4 minutes. Remove from the skillet and set aside.

**INCREASE** the heat under the skillet to medium-high and add the avocado oil. Working in batches if necessary, so as not to overcrowd the skillet, add the chicken in a single layer and cook until the chicken is golden brown and cooked through, 3 to 4 minutes per side.

**ADD** the white parts of the green onions to the skillet and cook, tossing, until the onions just begin to soften, about 2 minutes. Reduce the heat to medium.

**WHISK** the sauce once more, then pour it into the skillet. Cook, stirring, until the sauce thickens, and the chicken is well coated, about 3 more minutes.

**ADD** the green parts of the green onions and the toasted cashews to the skillet and toss to combine once more.

**IF** desired, serve with prepared rice. Garnish with more cashews and a lime wedge.

# slow cooker or pressure cooker creamy enchilada chicken

GLUTEN-FREE

PALEO

WHOLE30

GRAIN-FREE

**MAKES 4 SERVINGS** • **TOTAL TIME: 45 MINUTES OR 4 TO 6 HOURS**

2 pounds boneless, skinless chicken breasts, cut into 1-inch cubes

2 cups diced yellow onion (about 1 large onion)

4 garlic cloves, minced

2 tablespoons extra-virgin olive oil

2 teaspoons kosher salt

1 teaspoon freshly ground black pepper

1 tablespoon chili powder

1 teaspoon ground cumin

1 teaspoon onion powder

1 teaspoon dried oregano

1 teaspoon paprika

½ teaspoon cayenne pepper, optional

¾ cup low-sodium chicken broth

One 6-ounce can tomato paste

1 bay leaf

½ cup unsweetened full-fat coconut milk

1 tablespoon tapioca flour

2 tablespoons freshly squeezed lime juice (about 1 lime)

### FOR SERVING

Prepared steamed rice (sub cauliflower rice for Whole30, paleo, and grain-free)

1 lime, cut into wedges

Thinly sliced jalapeño, optional

Fresh cilantro leaves, for garnish

*If you love recipes in which you throw all the ingredients into a slow cooker or pressure cooker, then you're in for a treat! This easy recipe is a family favorite, and one that requires little effort for delicious results.*

## SLOW COOKER METHOD

IN a slow cooker, combine the chicken, onion, garlic, oil, salt, black pepper, chili powder, cumin, onion powder, oregano, paprika, cayenne (if using), broth, and tomato paste. Stir to combine. Place the bay leaf on top and cook on high for 4 hours or low for 6 hours. Discard the bay leaf.

WHEN the cook time is complete, in a medium bowl, whisk together the coconut milk and tapioca flour. Add the mixture and the lime juice to the slow cooker and stir to combine. Let sit, uncovered and on warm, to let the sauce thicken further, about 10 minutes, stirring occasionally.

SERVE over prepared rice with lime wedges. Garnish with jalapeños (if using) and cilantro.

## PRESSURE COOKER METHOD

IN the pressure cooker, combine the chicken, onion, garlic, oil, salt, black pepper, chili powder, cumin, onion powder, oregano, paprika, cayenne (if using), broth, and tomato paste. Stir to combine. Place the bay leaf on top.

LOCK the lid on the pressure cooker and turn the vent to "seal." Press the "manual" or "pressure cook" button (depending on your model) and set the time to 20 minutes.

WHEN the cook time is complete, quick-release the pressure. When all the pressure has been released, carefully remove the lid. Discard the bay leaf.

IN a medium bowl, whisk together the coconut milk and tapioca flour. Add the mixture and the lime juice to the pressure cooker with the cooked chicken. Stir until fully combined. Keep the setting on "warm" and the pot uncovered until the sauce has thickened, about 10 more minutes, stirring occasionally.

SERVE over prepared rice with lime wedges. Garnish with jalapeños (if using) and cilantro.

# skillet chicken and veggies with "peanut" sauce

**MAKES 4 SERVINGS** • **TOTAL TIME: 45 MINUTES**

## FOR THE "PEANUT" SAUCE

2 garlic cloves, roughly chopped

2 tablespoons Thai red curry paste

¼ cup unsweetened creamy almond butter

½ cup unsweetened full-fat coconut milk

1 teaspoon fish sauce (I use Red Boat brand)

2 tablespoons freshly squeezed lime juice (about 1 lime)

## FOR THE CHICKEN

4 small boneless, skinless chicken breasts

1 teaspoon kosher salt

½ teaspoon freshly ground black pepper

2 tablespoons avocado oil

## FOR THE VEGGIES

1 tablespoon avocado oil (if needed)

1-inch piece fresh ginger, peeled and finely grated

1 medium red bell pepper, sliced into ¼-inch-wide strips

1 cup halved and thinly sliced red onion (about ½ onion)

4 cups broccoli florets (about 1 head)

8 ounces sugar snap peas

½ teaspoon kosher salt

## FOR SERVING

¼ cup roughly chopped unsalted roasted cashews

¼ cup roughly chopped fresh cilantro

1 lime, cut into wedges

*Inspired by the flavors of chicken satay and peanut sauce, this dinner is the perfect one-skillet, simple weeknight dinner that is packed with flavor. The "peanut" sauce—which is actually made with almond butter to keep things Whole30—is a total showstopper with vibrant, complex flavors that make this dinner irresistible.*

PREHEAT the oven to 400°F.

MAKE THE "PEANUT" SAUCE: In a blender or using an immersion blender in a wide-mouth jar, combine the sauce ingredients and blend until smooth. (See the note for storing tips.)

PREPARE THE CHICKEN: Place the chicken breasts on a cutting board and cover with parchment paper or plastic wrap and use a meat mallet or the bottom of a heavy skillet to pound the chicken to a uniform ½-inch thickness. Pat dry with a paper towel and season both sides of the chicken with the salt and black pepper.

IN a large ovenproof skillet, heat the avocado oil over medium-high heat. Working in batches if necessary, so as not to overcrowd the skillet, place the chicken in the skillet and cook until golden brown on both sides, 3 to 4 minutes per side. The chicken doesn't need to be fully cooked through, as it will finish cooking in the oven. Transfer to a plate and set aside.

COOK THE VEGGIES: If the skillet is dry, add another tablespoon of avocado oil. Add the ginger, bell pepper, onion, broccoli, snap peas, and salt and sauté, stirring, for 2 minutes. Remove from the heat and drizzle ¼ cup of the sauce over the veggies. Stir to combine. Nestle the chicken on top of the veggies and spoon 2 teaspoons of the sauce over each chicken breast and spread it so that it evenly coats the top.

TRANSFER to the oven and bake until the chicken is cooked through and the broccoli is tender, 10 to 12 minutes.

GARNISH the skillet with the cashews and cilantro. Serve with extra sauce and lime wedges.

## FROM MY KITCHEN TO YOURS

The "peanut" sauce does not keep well in the fridge, as the coconut milk in it will thicken and harden. If you are meal-prepping and need to store it in the fridge, you may need to loosen up the sauce by setting it out at room temperature before serving or adding a splash of warm water and stirring until the sauce is loosened up.

# jerk-inspired chicken tacos

**MAKES 4 SERVINGS** • **TOTAL TIME: 35 MINUTES**

GLUTEN-FREE

GRAIN-FREE

*if modified:*
DAIRY-FREE
PALEO
WHOLE30

### FOR THE PINEAPPLE PICO

1 cup small-diced pineapple

¼ cup seeded and finely diced jalapeño

¼ cup finely diced red onion (about ¼ small onion)

1 tablespoon avocado oil

2 tablespoons freshly squeezed lime juice (about 1 lime)

¼ teaspoon kosher salt

¼ teaspoon freshly ground black pepper

### FOR THE AVOCADO MASH

1 large ripe avocado, halved and pitted

¼ cup freshly squeezed lime juice (about 2 limes)

¼ cup 2% or whole-milk Greek yogurt (sub nondairy sour cream for dairy-free, paleo, and Whole30)

2 tablespoons chopped fresh cilantro leaves

1 garlic clove, minced

¼ teaspoon kosher salt

### FOR THE CHICKEN

2 tablespoons avocado oil

4 cups shredded cooked chicken

1 teaspoon dried thyme

1 teaspoon ground allspice

½ teaspoon cayenne pepper

½ teaspoon garlic powder

½ teaspoon ground ginger

¾ teaspoon kosher salt

¼ teaspoon freshly ground black pepper

¼ cup low-sodium chicken broth

1 tablespoon freshly squeezed lime juice (about ½ lime)

### FOR THE TACOS

8 grain-free tortillas or lettuce cups

Chopped fresh cilantro, for garnish

1 lime, cut into wedges, for serving

*Taco Tuesday just got a little jerk twist! While a true Jamaican jerk chicken would involve cooking chicken over an open fire built out of wood from a pimento tree, this rendition uses shredded chicken flavored with a kicky homemade spice blend. The warming spices here pair beautifully with the pineapple pico and creamy avocado mash. Also, while any cooked, shredded chicken will work, you can save lots of time preparing these tacos with a rotisserie chicken!*

**MAKE THE PINEAPPLE PICO:** In a medium bowl, combine the pico ingredients and stir to combine. Set aside.

**MAKE THE AVOCADO MASH:** Scoop the avocado into a medium bowl and add the lime juice, yogurt, cilantro, garlic, and salt. Using the back of a fork, mash the avocado and stir to combine with the other ingredients until mostly smooth. Set aside.

**PREPARE THE CHICKEN:** In a large skillet, heat the oil over medium heat. Add the chicken, thyme, allspice, cayenne, garlic powder, ground ginger, salt, and black pepper and stir until the chicken is well coated in the spices. Spread the chicken in a single layer across the skillet. Cook, undisturbed, until a golden crust has formed, 3 to 4 minutes. Add the broth and lime juice and toss to combine. Continue to cook, stirring, until the chicken has mostly absorbed the broth, 2 to 3 minutes. Reduce the heat to low to keep warm while you warm the tortillas.

**ASSEMBLE THE TACOS:** If using tortillas, one at a time, place the tortillas in a dry (no oil) skillet over medium heat and heat them for about 30 seconds on each side. You can also use tongs to char the tortillas directly over a gas flame for a few seconds.

**FOR** each taco, smear a small amount of the avocado mash on a warm tortilla (or inside a lettuce cup) and fill it with the chicken. Garnish with pineapple pico and cilantro. Serve with lime wedges.

# chicken piccata meatballs

**MAKES 4 SERVINGS • TOTAL TIME: 40 MINUTES**

## FOR THE MEATBALLS

1½ pounds ground dark meat chicken or turkey

1 teaspoon kosher salt

½ teaspoon freshly ground black pepper

½ teaspoon garlic powder

2 tablespoons finely chopped fresh parsley leaves

¼ cup gluten-free panko bread crumbs (I use Aleia's brand)

1 egg yolk

Grated zest of ½ lemon

2 tablespoons extra-virgin olive oil

## FOR THE SAUCE

2 tablespoons unsalted butter (sub vegan butter for dairy-free)

3 garlic cloves, minced

½ teaspoon crushed red pepper flakes

½ teaspoon kosher salt

¼ teaspoon freshly ground black pepper

1 tablespoon cassava flour

¼ cup dry white wine

1¼ cups low-sodium chicken broth

2 tablespoons capers, drained

2 tablespoons freshly squeezed lemon juice (about 1 lemon)

1 tablespoon finely chopped fresh parsley leaves

## FOR SERVING

Chopped fresh parsley

Lemon wedges

*Chicken piccata is one of my absolute favorite go-to dinners. I mean, what is not to love about chicken drenched in a luscious white wine sauce that's brightened even more by lemon juice? I have a more traditional version of chicken piccata in my first book, but this meatball rendition has slowly become the fan favorite at my house and on my blog! This is an absolute crowd-pleasing dinner that you can serve however you please. Our favorite way? Over some brown rice linguine pasta!*

**PREPARE THE MEATBALLS:** In a large bowl, combine the ground chicken, salt, black pepper, garlic powder, parsley, panko, egg yolk, and lemon zest and mix well. Form the mixture into 1½-inch meatballs, dampening your hands as needed to make it easier to work with the mixture.

IN a large deep skillet, heat the oil over medium heat. Working in batches as needed, add the meatballs in a single layer and brown them on all sides, about 3 minutes per side. The meatballs do not need to be cooked all the way through, as they will finish cooking in the sauce. Set the browned meatballs aside on a plate.

**MAKE THE SAUCE:** In the same skillet, reduce the heat to medium-low and melt the butter. Add the garlic, pepper flakes, salt, black pepper, and cassava flour and whisk to combine, toasting the flour for 1 minute. Continue whisking and pour the wine into the skillet. Rapidly whisk until the sauce is smooth and thick. Whisk in the broth until well combined. Stir in the capers and lemon juice and increase the heat to a rapid simmer.

REDUCE the heat to a light simmer and nestle the meatballs back into the sauce. Cover and cook until the meatballs are cooked through, 5 to 7 minutes. Add the parsley and stir once more.

GARNISH with additional parsley and serve with lemon wedges.

# greek-inspired chicken and orzo bake

*if modified:*
GLUTEN-FREE
DAIRY-FREE

**MAKES 4 SERVINGS • TOTAL TIME: 45 MINUTES**

1½ teaspoons kosher salt, divided

1½ teaspoons dried oregano, divided

½ teaspoon freshly ground black pepper

1 teaspoon paprika

½ teaspoon ground cumin

¼ teaspoon cayenne pepper

1½ pounds boneless, skinless chicken thighs, trimmed of excess fat

2 tablespoons extra-virgin olive oil

2 garlic cloves, minced

½ cup thinly sliced shallot (about 1 large shallot)

1 bunch asparagus, woody ends trimmed, cut into 2-inch pieces

2 cups halved cherry tomatoes

½ cup dry white wine

¾ cup orzo (sub gluten-free orzo for gluten-free)

One 14-ounce can quartered artichoke hearts, drained

1 cup low-sodium chicken broth

½ cup pitted kalamata olives

½ cup crumbled feta cheese (omit for dairy-free)

2 tablespoons chopped fresh parsley leaves

*Boldly seasoned chicken, crisp asparagus, juicy tomatoes, and orzo come together for a healthy and delicious Greek-inspired dinner. The soft and pillowy orzo really soaks up all the delicious Mediterranean flavors and rounds out this simple, mouthwatering, one-skillet dinner.*

PREHEAT the oven to 400°F.

IN a small bowl, combine 1 teaspoon of the salt, ½ teaspoon of the oregano, the black pepper, paprika, cumin, and cayenne. Pat the chicken dry and season with the spice blend on both sides evenly.

IN a large deep ovenproof skillet (preferably cast-iron), heat the oil over medium-high heat. Working in batches if necessary, so as not to overcrowd the skillet, add the chicken in a single layer and cook until golden brown on both sides, about 2 minutes per side. Transfer the browned chicken to a plate and set aside. The chicken does not have to be cooked through as it will finish in the oven.

REDUCE the heat beneath the skillet to medium, add the garlic, shallot, asparagus, cherry tomatoes, and remaining ½ teaspoon salt. Cook, stirring, until the tomatoes begin to soften and the asparagus turns bright green, about 4 minutes.

POUR in the wine and deglaze the skillet, scraping up any browned bits from the bottom. Cook, stirring, until the wine is reduced by half, about 2 minutes. Add the orzo, artichoke hearts, broth, and remaining 1 teaspoon oregano and stir to combine. Bring the mixture to a simmer, then nestle the browned chicken into the skillet and sprinkle the olives over the entire skillet.

TRANSFER to the oven and bake, uncovered, for 10 minutes. Remove from the oven and crumble the feta (if using) over the chicken. Return to the oven and bake until the chicken is cooked through and the orzo is tender, 10 to 12 more minutes.

LET cool for 5 minutes before serving. Garnish with the fresh parsley.

# ginger and peanut butter ground turkey stir-fry

**MAKES 4 SERVINGS** • **TOTAL TIME: 25 MINUTES**

## FOR THE STIR-FRY

2 tablespoons avocado oil

¼ cup minced shallot (about 1 large shallot)

2 garlic cloves, minced

1-inch piece fresh ginger, peeled and finely grated

2 pounds ground turkey, preferably dark meat

1½ teaspoons kosher salt

½ teaspoon freshly ground black pepper

2 tablespoons creamy peanut butter (sub unsweetened almond butter for Whole30)

2 tablespoons coconut aminos

1 tablespoon rice vinegar

½ teaspoon toasted sesame oil

2 tablespoons freshly squeezed lime juice (about 1 lime)

2 tablespoons no-sugar-added sriracha (I use Yellowbird brand)

4 green onions, thinly sliced

## FOR SERVING

Prepared steamed rice (sub cauliflower rice for Whole30, paleo, and grain-free)

Fresh mint leaves

Fresh Thai basil leaves

Fresh cilantro leaves

*Not only is this recipe ridiculously delicious, but it is also quick and easy to make. Ground turkey gets a bad rep for being dry and bland, but here it's filled with umami flavors, a touch of creamy peanut butter, and a zip of ginger to make it anything but bland. I have a strong feeling it's going to become your new go-to dinner!*

IN a large nonstick skillet, heat the oil over medium heat. Add the shallot, garlic, and ginger and cook, stirring often, until the shallot begins to soften, about 2 minutes.

ADD the turkey, salt, and pepper and cook, breaking up the meat with the edge of a spoon, until it is cooked through and no longer pink, about 7 minutes.

MEANWHILE, in a small bowl, combine the peanut butter, coconut aminos, rice vinegar, toasted sesame oil, lime juice, and sriracha. Whisk until well combined and smooth.

POUR the sauce into the ground turkey mixture and add the sliced green onions. Cook, stirring, until the turkey is well coated and the green onions are just tender, about 3 more minutes.

SERVE over prepared rice. Garnish with fresh herbs.

135 CAJUN SAUSAGE AND RICE SKILLET

136 ITALIAN SKIRT STEAK WITH BURSTING TOMATOES

139 SLOW COOKER OR PRESSURE COOKER GOCHUJANG SHREDDED BEEF BOWLS

143 SHEET PAN SAUSAGE AND SWEET PIQUANTÉ PEPPERS

144 SIMPLE SKILLET BEEF SHAWARMA

147 HERBY MEDITERRANEAN BAKED MEATBALLS

148 LEMONGRASS PORK LETTUCE CUPS

150 ZA'ATAR-CRUSTED LAMB CHOPS WITH ROASTED CARROTS AND HERB DRIZZLE

153 PHILLY CHEESESTEAK–STUFFED MUSHROOMS

154 CHILI OIL PORK AND CABBAGE STIR-FRY

156 CRUNCHY BAKED BEEF TACOS

159 SHEET PAN MINI BBQ-CHEDDAR MEATLOAVES WITH SWEET POTATOES AND BRUSSELS SPROUTS

160 SKILLET MOJO PORK TENDERLOIN

163 EASY GROUND LAMB CURRY

164 BEEF ENCHILADA–STUFFED ACORN SQUASH

167 SICHUAN-INSPIRED BEEF STIR-FRY

beef, pork, and lamb

# cajun sausage and rice skillet

GLUTEN-FREE

DAIRY-FREE

MAKES 4 SERVINGS  •  TOTAL TIME: 45 MINUTES

¼ teaspoon cayenne pepper, or more to taste

1 teaspoon smoked paprika

1 teaspoon dried oregano

1 teaspoon dried thyme

1 teaspoon dried rosemary

1 teaspoon kosher salt

½ teaspoon freshly ground black pepper

2 tablespoons extra-virgin olive oil

12 ounces andouille sausage, thinly sliced on the diagonal

1 cup finely diced yellow onion (about ½ small onion)

½ cup finely diced celery (about 1 stalk)

1 cup small-diced green bell pepper

2 garlic cloves, minced

½ cup dry white wine

1 cup medium-grain white rice, rinsed well and drained

One 14.5-ounce can diced fire-roasted tomatoes

¾ cup low-sodium chicken broth

1 bay leaf

3 green onions, thinly sliced on the diagonal

1 tablespoon freshly squeezed lemon juice (about ½ lemon)

Chopped fresh parsley, optional for serving

*This one-pan, Cajun-inspired dinner is a wonderful way to spice up your weeknight. It borrows similar flavors and ingredients from jambalaya, but it's a slightly scaled-back, simplified version. To make this meal taste best, I recommend finding andouille sausage, a smoked pork sausage commonly used in Louisiana-style cooking. If you can't find it, kielbasa sausage will work just fine!*

IN a small bowl, combine the cayenne, smoked paprika, oregano, thyme, rosemary, salt, and black pepper. Set aside.

IN a large deep skillet, heat the oil over medium-high heat. Add the sausage and spread it into a single layer. Cook, undisturbed, until the sausage is browned on one side, about 2 minutes. Toss and cook for 2 more minutes to further brown the sausage. Use a slotted spoon to remove the sausage to a plate. Set aside.

REDUCE the heat to medium and add the onion, celery, bell pepper, and garlic to the skillet. Cook, stirring, until the vegetables are slightly softened, about 4 minutes. Add the spice mixture and cook, stirring and toasting the spices until fragrant, about 2 minutes.

POUR the wine into the skillet and stir, scraping up any browned bits on the bottom of the pan. Simmer until the wine has reduced by half, about 2 minutes.

ADD the rice, tomatoes, and broth and stir to combine. Add the bay leaf and bring to a simmer. Reduce the heat to medium-low, nestle the sausage back into the skillet with the rice, cover, and cook at a light simmer for 20 minutes. Remove the skillet from the heat and keep covered for 10 minutes to let the rice steam until tender.

FLUFF the rice with a fork and stir in the green onions and lemon juice. Divide among bowls and garnish with chopped parsley, if desired.

# italian skirt steak with bursting tomatoes

**MAKES 4 SERVINGS** • **TOTAL TIME: 30 MINUTES**

## FOR THE STEAK

1½ pounds skirt steak (see note) or flap steak

1½ teaspoons kosher salt

1 teaspoon freshly ground black pepper

1 teaspoon dried oregano

2 tablespoons extra-virgin olive oil

## FOR THE BLISTERED TOMATOES

½ cup halved and thinly sliced shallot (about 1 large shallot)

4 garlic cloves, thinly sliced

½ teaspoon crushed red pepper flakes, optional

¼ cup low-sodium beef broth or chicken broth

2 cups cherry tomatoes (or 1 pint)

2 tablespoons freshly squeezed lemon juice (about 1 lemon)

½ cup roughly chopped fresh parsley leaves

¼ cup thinly sliced fresh basil leaves, plus more for garnish (optional)

*The wonderful thing about cooking with skirt steak is that you don't need a thermometer to ensure it's done. When cooked in a hot skillet, the inside will be medium-rare once the steak has a deep, dark-brown sear on the outsides. The steak is seasoned simply here, but the magic is in the bright, bursting tomatoes with fresh herbs.*

**PREPARE THE STEAK:** Place the steak on a cutting board and cut it with the grain into 6-inch-wide pieces (this makes it easier to fit into your skillet). Trim any excess fat. Pat dry with a paper towel and season both sides of the pieces with the salt, black pepper, and oregano. Press the seasoning into the meat to adhere and set aside.

**IN** a large stainless steel skillet, heat the oil over medium-high heat. Once the oil is hot, carefully add the steak. Depending on the size of your skillet, you may need to do this in batches so as not to overcrowd the pan. Cook, undisturbed, until a golden-brown crust forms on each side, 3 to 4 minutes per side. Transfer to a cutting board, tent with foil, and set aside to rest.

**MAKE THE BLISTERED TOMATOES:** Using the same skillet, reduce the heat to medium. Add the shallot, garlic, pepper flakes (if using), and broth and cook, scraping up the browned bits on the bottom of the pan, until the shallot and garlic begin to soften, about 2 minutes. Add the tomatoes and increase the heat to medium-high. Toss to combine and cook, stirring often, until the tomatoes begin to burst, about 4 minutes. Remove from the heat and stir in the lemon juice, parsley, and basil.

**SLICE** the steak thinly against the grain and transfer to a serving platter with its juices. Spoon the tomato mixture over the steak, garnish with additional basil, if desired, and serve.

## FROM MY KITCHEN TO YOURS

There are two types of skirt steak: the inside skirt and the outside skirt. If it's not clearly labeled at your grocery store, be sure to ask your butcher; the outside skirt is much more desirable as it is more tender and less coarse. If only the inside skirt is available, tenderize it with a meat mallet or the bottom of a heavy skillet to a uniform ¼-inch thickness.

# slow cooker or pressure cooker gochujang shredded beef bowls

GLUTEN-FREE

DAIRY-FREE

PALEO

GRAIN-FREE

**MAKES 6 SERVINGS** • **TOTAL TIME: 1 HOUR OR 4 TO 8 HOURS**

## FOR THE STEAK

2½ pounds flank or flap steak, trimmed of excess fat

2 teaspoons kosher salt

1 teaspoon freshly ground black pepper

2 tablespoons tapioca flour

2 tablespoons avocado oil

## FOR THE SAUCE

¾ cup coconut aminos

⅓ cup gochujang (I use Mother In Law's brand; sub a gluten-free brand for gluten-free, see page 6)

2 tablespoons toasted sesame oil

2 tablespoons apple cider vinegar

2-inch piece fresh ginger, peeled and finely grated

4 garlic cloves, minced

⅓ cup coconut sugar

⅓ cup low-sodium beef broth (for the pressure cooker method)

## FOR SERVING

1½ cups prepared cauliflower rice or steamed rice

1 cup kimchi (I use Wildbrine brand)

4 radishes, very thinly sliced

4 green onions, thinly sliced on the diagonal

1 avocado, sliced

2 tablespoons toasted sesame seeds

*This Korean-inspired beef bowl is absolutely delicious. The gochujang-infused beef is tender and juicy on the inside and crisp on the edges, making it the perfect protein with endless opportunities to customize. Whether it is served over a rice bowl, as I did here, or it's going into tacos, lettuce wraps, or even on a salad, this beef is a delicious option for meal prep and busy weekdays when you want to set it and forget it!*

### SLOW COOKER METHOD

PREPARE THE STEAK: Cut the steak into 4 equal pieces. Pat dry with a paper towel and season both sides of each piece with the salt and pepper.

POUR the tapioca flour in a large shallow bowl. Dredge the steak in the flour to coat both sides.

IN a large skillet, heat the avocado oil over medium-high heat. When the oil is hot, working in batches so as not to overcrowd the pan, sear the beef on both sides until a deep brown crust forms, 3 to 4 minutes per side. Transfer to a plate. Once all of the steak has been seared, transfer the steak and any juices to the slow cooker.

MAKE THE SAUCE: In a medium bowl, combine the coconut aminos, gochujang, sesame oil, vinegar, ginger, garlic, and coconut sugar. Whisk until well combined. Transfer ½ cup of the sauce to a small bowl, cover, and refrigerate (you'll use this as a sauce for serving). Pour the remaining sauce over the browned beef in the slow cooker. Cover and cook on high for 4 hours or low for 6 to 8 hours, until the beef is fall-apart tender.

USING tongs, transfer the beef to a sheet pan. Do not dispose of the liquid remaining in the slow cooker. Using two forks, shred the beef. Ladle 1 cup of the liquid from the slow cooker over the beef, toss to coat, and spread into a single layer on the sheet pan.

PLACE the sheet pan on the top rack of the oven and turn the oven to broil (set to high if you have the option). If you don't have a broiler, heat the oven to 500°F or as hot as you can set it. Broil or bake until the beef

*(recipe continues)*

begins to crisp up on the edges, 3 to 5 minutes, depending on how hot your broiler gets, watching carefully as it crisps to make sure it doesn't burn.

SERVE with the prepared rice and kimchi. Drizzle each serving with some of the reserved sauce. Top with radishes, green onions, avocado, and a sprinkle of sesame seeds, if desired.

### PRESSURE COOKER METHOD

PREPARE THE STEAK: Cut the steak into 4 equal pieces. Pat dry with a paper towel and season both sides of each piece with the salt and pepper.

POUR the tapioca flour into a large, shallow bowl. Dredge the steak in the flour to coat both sides.

TURN the pressure cooker on the "sauté" function and add the oil. When the oil is hot, working in batches so as not to overcrowd the pot, sear the beef on both sides until a deep brown crust forms, 3 to 4 minutes per side. Transfer to a plate. When all the pieces have been seared, hit "cancel," and return the steak and any juices to the pressure cooker.

MAKE THE SAUCE: In a medium bowl, combine the coconut aminos, gochujang, sesame oil, vinegar, ginger, garlic, and coconut sugar. Whisk until well combined. Transfer ½ cup of the sauce to a small bowl, cover, and refrigerate (you'll use this as a sauce for serving). Pour the remaining sauce over the browned beef in the pressure cooker, then pour in the broth.

LOCK the lid of the pressure cooker and turn the vent to "seal." Press the "manual" or "pressure cook" button (depending on your model) and set the time to 45 minutes. Walk away from the pressure cooker and let it do its thing!

ONCE the cook time is finished, quick-release the pressure. When all the pressure has been released, carefully remove the lid and use tongs to transfer the beef to a sheet pan. Do not dispose of the liquid remaining in the pressure cooker. Using two forks, shred the beef. Ladle 1 cup of the cooking liquid from the pressure cooker over the beef, toss to coat, and spread into a single layer on the pan.

PLACE the sheet pan on the top rack of the oven and turn the oven to broil (set to high if you have the option). If you don't have a broiler, heat the oven to 500°F or as hot as you can set it. Broil or bake until the beef begins to crisp up on the edges, 3 to 5 minutes, depending on how hot your broiler gets, watching carefully as it crisps to make sure it doesn't burn.

SERVE with the prepared rice and kimchi. Drizzle each serving with some of the reserved sauce. Top with radishes, green onions, avocado, and a sprinkle of sesame seeds, if desired.

# sheet pan sausage and sweet piquanté peppers

MAKES 4 SERVINGS • TOTAL TIME: 25 MINUTES

GLUTEN-FREE

GRAIN-FREE

*if modified:*
DAIRY-FREE

## FOR THE PESTO SAUCE

⅓ cup store-bought basil pesto or Lemon Basil Pesto (page 8)

⅓ cup extra-virgin olive oil

Grated zest of ½ lemon

2 tablespoons freshly squeezed lemon juice (about 1 lemon)

## FOR THE SHEET PAN

1 cup piquanté peppers, drained

4 hot or mild Italian sausage links

4 cups cauliflower florets (about 1 small head)

1 tablespoon extra-virgin olive oil

½ teaspoon kosher salt

½ teaspoon freshly ground black pepper

½ cup roughly chopped walnuts

2 ounces goat cheese, crumbled (omit for dairy-free)

¼ cup julienned fresh basil, optional for garnish

*This is the ultimate weeknight dinner recipe. All you need is one pan and a handful of ready-to-use ingredients. Store-bought hot Italian sausage is roasted with cauliflower and an herbaceous pesto drizzle with a bright pop of flavor from piquanté peppers, commonly known as Peppadews. If you've never had a piquanté pepper before, they'll quickly become a favorite. A little bit sweet, a little bit spicy, and with quite a bit of pickled tang, they add the perfect punch to this simple sheet pan dinner and pair beautifully with the creamy goat cheese crumbles.*

PREHEAT the oven to 400°F. Line a sheet pan with parchment paper.

MAKE THE PESTO SAUCE: In a medium bowl, whisk together the pesto sauce ingredients. Set aside.

PREPARE THE SHEET PAN: Place the piquantés on a plate lined with paper towels to remove any excess moisture. Set aside.

ARRANGE the sausage links on the prepared sheet pan and scatter the cauliflower around the links. Pour ½ cup of the pesto sauce and the oil over everything, then sprinkle with the salt and black pepper. Gently toss to coat. Bake for 10 minutes.

REMOVE the pan from the oven and flip the sausages. Add the piquantés and walnuts to the pan and drizzle another ¼ cup pesto sauce over the piquantés, walnuts, and cauliflower. Gently toss, then return to the oven for 10 minutes.

REMOVE from the oven and let the sheet pan mixture cool for 3 to 5 minutes, then crumble the goat cheese (if using) over the pan.

DIVIDE the sausages and accompaniments among four plates. Drizzle with the remaining pesto sauce and garnish with fresh basil, if desired.

# simple skillet beef shawarma

**MAKES 4 SERVINGS** • **TOTAL TIME: 55 MINUTES**

## FOR THE STEAK

1½ pounds flap or skirt steak, trimmed of excess fat

3 tablespoons extra-virgin olive oil, divided, plus more as needed

1 tablespoon apple cider vinegar

1 tablespoon tapioca flour

1 teaspoon ground cumin

1 teaspoon paprika

1 teaspoon kosher salt

½ teaspoon freshly ground black pepper

½ teaspoon garlic powder

¼ teaspoon ground allspice

¼ teaspoon cayenne pepper

¼ teaspoon ground cinnamon

## FOR THE TAHINI DRIZZLE

3 tablespoons tahini

2 tablespoons plain 2% or whole-milk Greek yogurt (sub nondairy sour cream for dairy-free, paleo, and Whole30)

2 tablespoons freshly squeezed lemon juice (about 1 lemon)

¼ teaspoon kosher salt

1 garlic clove, minced

## OPTIONAL FOR SERVING

Pita bread, warmed (omit for gluten-free, paleo, Whole30, and grain-free)

Feta, crumbled (omit for dairy-free, paleo, and Whole30)

Thinly sliced Roma (plum) tomato

Thinly sliced yellow onion

Thinly sliced romaine lettuce

Sliced dill pickles

Fresh parsley leaves

*This popular Middle Eastern street food is traditionally made on a vertical rotisserie or spit, where the meat is slow-roasted for days until perfectly tender and then shaved off and served in pita pockets. But you can make a terrific at-home version using a good skillet and a beautiful blend of spices. Of course, this beef shawarma is delicious served in pita pockets, but it's also great over a grain bowl or on top of salads (especially my Fattoush Salad, page 28), making it perfect for meal prep! No matter how you serve it, you'll be impressed with how flavorful and tender the meat is—and the tahini drizzle is tough to beat.*

**PREPARE THE STEAK:** Place the steak on a cutting board. Using a meat mallet or the bottom of a heavy skillet, pound the steak to an even ¼-inch thickness. Cutting against the grain, slice the steak into ½-inch-wide strips that are 2 to 3 inches long.

**PLACE** the sliced steak in a large bowl and add 1 tablespoon of the oil, the vinegar, tapioca flour, cumin, paprika, salt, black pepper, garlic powder, allspice, cayenne, and cinnamon. Toss until well combined. Set aside to marinate at room temperature for 15 to 20 minutes.

**MEANWHILE, MAKE THE TAHINI DRIZZLE:** In a small bowl, combine the tahini, yogurt, lemon juice, salt, and garlic. Whisk until smooth. If the drizzle is too thick, add 1 to 2 tablespoons of warm water as needed until the sauce is smooth and creamy. Set aside.

**COOK THE STEAK:** In a large nonstick skillet, heat the remaining 2 tablespoons oil over medium-high heat. Working in batches so as not to overcrowd the skillet, sear the beef until a golden-brown crust begins to form, 2 to 3 minutes per side. Transfer the cooked beef to a plate. If the skillet runs dry as you're crisping the meat, add more oil as needed.

**TO SERVE:** I often serve this family-style, as pictured, with the various serving options so everyone can build their pitas or bowls as desired.

# herby mediterranean baked meatballs

GLUTEN-FREE

GRAIN-FREE

**MAKES 6 SERVINGS** • **TOTAL TIME: 1 HOUR**

Extra-virgin olive oil for the baking dish

### FOR THE YOGURT SAUCE

½ cup plain 2% or whole-milk Greek yogurt

¼ cup chopped fresh parsley

¼ cup chopped fresh dill

2 garlic cloves, minced

Grated zest of ½ lemon

2 tablespoons freshly squeezed lemon juice (about 1 lemon)

½ teaspoon kosher salt

### FOR THE MEATBALLS

1 pound ground beef (90/10)

1 pound ground lamb

2 tablespoons tapioca flour

1 teaspoon paprika

1 teaspoon kosher salt

1 teaspoon freshly ground black pepper

½ teaspoon ground cumin

½ teaspoon ground coriander

½ teaspoon crushed red pepper flakes

¼ cup chopped fresh parsley

2 garlic cloves, minced

Grated zest of ½ lemon

1 large egg, whisked

### FOR THE HARISSA-TOMATO SAUCE

One 13.8-ounce carton chopped tomatoes

½ cup mild harissa

½ teaspoon ground cumin

½ teaspoon kosher salt

### TO FINISH

2 ounces feta cheese, crumbled

2 tablespoons pine nuts

1 teaspoon white wine vinegar

Small dill fronds, for garnish

*If you are familiar with the Epic Baked Meatballs in my previous cookbook and blog, you'll recognize these; they should really be called Epic Baked Meatballs 2.0. Lamb and beef meatballs are infused with yogurt and herbs, then covered with an easy harissa-tomato sauce. They've got a little bit of heat, a lot of herby flavor, and a little tang from the yogurt sauce served on top. They're outstanding and pair well with roasted vegetables, a big salad, and pita bread.*

PREHEAT the oven to 425°F. Use a paper towel to evenly coat the bottom of a 9 × 13-inch baking dish with a little oil.

MAKE THE YOGURT SAUCE: In a medium bowl, combine the yogurt, parsley, dill, garlic, lemon zest, lemon juice, and salt. Measure out ½ cup for the meatballs and place the rest in the fridge until ready to serve.

PREPARE THE MEATBALLS: In a large bowl, combine the ground beef, ground lamb, tapioca flour, paprika, salt, black pepper, cumin, coriander, pepper flakes, parsley, garlic, lemon zest, egg, and the reserved ½ cup yogurt mixture. Using clean hands, mix the meat until just combined.

USING your hands, form the meat mixture into 2-inch balls. Place the meatballs in a single layer in the prepared baking dish. There should be 16 to 18 meatballs.

BAKE, uncovered, until the meatballs are browned, about 20 minutes.

MEANWHILE, MAKE THE HARISSA-TOMATO SAUCE: In a medium bowl, combine the tomatoes, harissa, cumin, and salt. Set aside.

TO FINISH: Carefully remove the meatballs from the oven and drain off any excess fat. Reduce the oven temperature to 325°F. Pour the harissa-tomato sauce evenly over the meatballs. Crumble the feta over the top and sprinkle evenly with the pine nuts.

RETURN to the oven and bake, uncovered, until the meatballs are tender and no longer pink in the center and the sauce is very hot and bubbling, about 20 minutes. Let cool for 5 to 10 minutes.

STIR the vinegar into the reserved yogurt sauce, then drizzle the yogurt sauce over the meatballs. Top with dill fronds for garnish.

# lemongrass pork lettuce cups

**MAKES 4 SERVINGS** • **TOTAL TIME: 45 MINUTES**

### FOR THE PORK

2 pounds pork tenderloin

2 tablespoons avocado oil

3 tablespoons coconut aminos

2 tablespoons fish sauce (I use Red Boat brand)

½ teaspoon toasted sesame oil

2 garlic cloves, minced

2 teaspoons minced fresh ginger

2 tablespoons minced lemongrass (about 2 stalks lemongrass, tender white inner bulb only; see note)

Grated zest of ½ lime

1 teaspoon kosher salt

½ teaspoon freshly ground black pepper

1 tablespoon coconut sugar (omit for Whole30)

1 tablespoon tapioca flour

3 Thai chiles, minced, optional

### FOR THE QUICK-PICKLED VEGGIES

1 cup matchstick-cut carrots (about ½ medium carrot)

1 cup halved and thinly sliced radishes

½ cup halved and thinly sliced shallot (about 1 large shallot)

¼ cup rice vinegar

¼ teaspoon kosher salt

### FOR THE SPICY MAYO

2 tablespoons Homemade Mayo (page 7)

2 teaspoons no-sugar-added sriracha (I use Yellowbird brand)

1 tablespoon freshly squeezed lime juice (about ½ lime)

*Inspired by the flavors of banh mi, a Vietnamese sandwich that typically consists of a baguette, pork, pickled vegetables, herbs, and chiles, this recipe includes seared pork served in lettuce leaves with quick-pickled veggies for a light and refreshing meal. If you're looking for something a little heartier, serve this over rice instead of in lettuce cups. You can also easily swap the pork for boneless, skinless chicken thighs or flap steak!*

**PREPARE THE PORK:** Using a sharp paring knife, remove the silver skin from the tenderloin. Cut the pork into 1-inch cubes and place them in a large bowl. Add the avocado oil, coconut aminos, fish sauce, sesame oil, garlic, ginger, lemongrass, lime zest, salt, pepper, coconut sugar (if using), tapioca flour, and Thai chiles (if using). Toss until the pork is well coated. Set aside to marinate for at least 15 minutes. (Alternatively, cover the bowl with plastic wrap and transfer to the fridge to marinate for up to 24 hours.)

**MEANWHILE, MAKE THE QUICK-PICKLED VEGGIES:** In a medium bowl, combine the pickled veggie ingredients. Toss to combine and set aside.

**MAKE THE SPICY MAYO:** In a small bowl, combine the spicy mayo ingredients. Set aside.

**TO FINISH:** In a large nonstick skillet, heat the avocado oil over medium heat until hot but not yet smoking. Working in batches so as not to overcrowd the skillet, carefully add the pork pieces in a single layer and cook, undisturbed, until a golden-brown crust forms on one side, about 3 minutes. Toss and continue to cook until the pork is cooked through, 3 to 4 more minutes. As you work, use a slotted spoon to transfer the cooked pork to a clean plate.

**TO ASSEMBLE** the cups, place a spoonful of the pork on two layered lettuce leaves. Top with some pickled veggies and a drizzle of the spicy mayo. Garnish with fresh mint leaves and/or cilantro leaves. Serve with lime wedges.

**2 tablespoons avocado oil**

**2 heads butter lettuce, separated into individual lettuce leaves, rinsed, and patted dry**

**Fresh mint leaves and/or cilantro leaves, torn**

**1 lime, cut into wedges, for serving**

## FROM MY KITCHEN TO YOURS

To mince a stalk of lemongrass, first trim off the spiky top and enough of the bottom so that you no longer see a woody core. Peel off a few of the outer layers until you're left with just the tender heart of the stalk. Next, slice the stalk thinly crosswise, then chop through the slices until they're minced.

# za'atar-crusted lamb chops with roasted carrots and herb drizzle

**MAKES 4 SERVINGS** • **TOTAL TIME: 45 MINUTES**

### FOR THE LAMB CHOPS

8 to 10 frenched lamb rib chops (about 1 inch thick; 2 pounds)

2 teaspoons za'atar seasoning (see note)

1 teaspoon kosher salt

1 teaspoon freshly ground black pepper

### FOR THE CARROTS

2 pounds rainbow carrots, peeled, ends trimmed, and halved or quartered lengthwise (depending on their size)

2 tablespoons extra-virgin olive oil

2 tablespoons pure maple syrup (omit for Whole30)

1 teaspoon smoked paprika

½ teaspoon ground cumin

1 teaspoon kosher salt

½ teaspoon freshly ground black pepper

### FOR THE HERB DRIZZLE

½ cup chopped fresh dill

½ cup chopped fresh cilantro

2 garlic cloves, roughly chopped

⅓ cup extra-virgin olive oil

1 tablespoon champagne vinegar

Grated zest of ½ lemon

1 tablespoon freshly squeezed lemon juice (about ½ lemon)

¼ teaspoon crushed red pepper flakes

½ teaspoon kosher salt

### TO FINISH

2 tablespoons extra-virgin olive oil, divided

Chopped fresh dill, optional for serving

*Za'atar, a Mediterranean spice blend, infuses flavor into the lamb for a simple yet elegant meal. Paired with sweet and smoky roasted carrots and an herb drizzle that really brightens up your entire plate, this is comfort food reimagined into an impressive meal.*

PREHEAT the oven to 400°F. Line a sheet pan with parchment paper.

SEASON THE LAMB CHOPS: Sprinkle the za'atar, salt, and black pepper on both sides of the lamb chops and massage the seasoning into the meat. Let the lamb sit for about 10 minutes at room temperature while you prepare the rest of the meal.

ROAST THE CARROTS: Lay the carrots on the prepared sheet pan, drizzle them with the oil and maple syrup, and sprinkle them with the smoked paprika, cumin, salt, and pepper. Toss to coat well, then arrange the carrots on the pan cut side down. Roast until tender, 20 to 25 minutes.

MEANWHILE, MAKE THE HERB DRIZZLE: In a blender or using an immersion blender in a wide-mouth jar, combine the drizzle ingredients and blend until mostly smooth. Set aside at room temperature until ready to serve.

TO FINISH: While the carrots roast, in a large skillet, heat 1 tablespoon of the oil over medium-high heat. Swirl the pan so that the oil coats the bottom evenly. When the oil is shimmering, working in batches so as not to overcrowd the skillet, sear half the lamb until a golden-brown crust begins to form, 2 to 3 minutes per side for medium-rare. Repeat with the remaining lamb chops, adding the remaining 1 tablespoon oil to coat the pan for the second batch. Transfer the lamb to a cutting board or platter and let rest for 5 minutes before serving.

SERVE family-style or divide the lamb chops and carrots among four plates and top with the herb drizzle. Garnish with more dill, if desired.

## FROM MY KITCHEN TO YOURS

Most store-bought za'atar seasonings have added salt. If yours does not, add an extra ½ teaspoon of salt to the lamb chops to ensure they are well seasoned.

# philly cheesesteak-stuffed mushrooms

**MAKES 4 SERVINGS** • **TOTAL TIME: 30 MINUTES**

## FOR THE MUSHROOMS

4 large portobello mushrooms

8 teaspoons extra-virgin olive oil

1 teaspoon kosher salt

## FOR THE FILLING

1 pound skirt or flap steak, cut into ¼-inch pieces

2 teaspoons tapioca flour

1 teaspoon kosher salt

½ teaspoon freshly ground black pepper

½ teaspoon cayenne pepper

½ teaspoon dried thyme

½ teaspoon garlic powder

2 tablespoons extra-virgin olive oil

¾ cup small-diced green bell pepper

½ cup small-diced yellow onion (about ½ small onion)

2 garlic cloves, minced

2 teaspoons Dijon mustard

2 tablespoons coconut aminos

½ teaspoon fish sauce (I use Red Boat brand)

4 slices provolone cheese

Chopped fresh parsley leaves, optional for garnish

*To me, a Philly cheesesteak is the ultimate hoagie sandwich. Done in just 30 minutes and loaded with flavor, this low-carb version has the flavors of the classic sandwich and is just fantastic!*

POSITION a rack in the center of the oven and turn the oven to high broil. If you don't have a broiler, turn your oven to its hottest setting.

GENTLY wipe the mushrooms clean with a damp paper towel. Remove the stem of each mushroom and discard. Using a small spoon, scrape out the gills of each mushroom and discard.

PLACE the mushrooms on a sheet pan. Drizzle 2 teaspoons of oil onto each mushroom, brushing it onto each side. Place gill side down and broil for 4 minutes. Remove from the oven and flip the mushrooms. Season inside each cap with ¼ teaspoon salt. Return to the oven and broil until tender, about 4 more minutes, watching carefully so as not to burn the mushrooms. Remove from the oven and set aside. Leave the broiler on.

MEANWHILE, PREPARE THE FILLING: Place the diced steak in a medium bowl and sprinkle with the tapioca flour, salt, black pepper, cayenne, thyme, and garlic powder. Toss until evenly coated.

IN a large nonstick skillet, heat the oil over medium-high heat. Add the meat in a single layer and cook, undisturbed, until a golden-brown crust is formed, about 2 minutes. Flip the meat and continue to cook until just cooked through, about 2 more minutes. Using a slotted spoon, transfer the browned meat to a clean plate. Set aside.

REDUCE the heat under the skillet to medium. Add the bell pepper, onion, and garlic and sauté, scraping up any browned bits left from the meat and stirring often, until the vegetables are just softened, 4 to 5 minutes.

RETURN the meat and any juices to the skillet. Add the mustard, coconut aminos, and fish sauce and toss until well combined. Remove from the heat.

DIVIDE the filling among the mushroom caps. Top each mushroom with 1 slice of provolone. Return to the oven and broil for 2 to 3 minutes to melt the cheese, watching carefully so as not to burn the cheese.

GARNISH with parsley, if desired.

# chili oil pork and cabbage stir-fry

**MAKES 4 SERVINGS** • **TOTAL TIME: 30 MINUTES**

### FOR THE CHILI OIL

4 garlic cloves, minced

1-inch piece fresh ginger, peeled and finely grated

1 teaspoon crushed red pepper flakes

1 teaspoon Sichuan peppercorns, crushed (I place them in a bag and crush using the back of a spoon)

½ teaspoon Chinese five-spice powder

¼ cup avocado oil

### FOR THE STIR-FRY

2 tablespoons avocado oil

1 pound ground pork

1 teaspoon kosher salt

1 small head green cabbage, hand-torn (see note)

2 green onions, thinly sliced on the diagonal

2 tablespoons rice vinegar

¼ cup coconut aminos

1 tablespoon coconut sugar (omit for Whole30)

1 teaspoon fish sauce (I use Red Boat brand)

*Inspired by two dishes that I love, chili oil dumplings and Chinese cabbage stir-fry, this recipe is filled with aromatic flavors and Sichuan peppercorns for a finish that's a little bit tangy and a little bit spicy. This cooks quickly, so be sure to have all the ingredients ready!*

**MAKE THE CHILI OIL:** In a wide-mouth jar, combine the garlic, ginger, pepper flakes, Sichuan peppercorns, and five-spice powder. In a large deep skillet or wok, heat the avocado oil over medium-high heat until sizzling hot and just beginning to lightly smoke. Very carefully pour the hot oil into the jar with the spice mixture and stir. It should sizzle and become fragrant. Set aside.

**MAKE THE STIR-FRY:** In the same skillet, heat the 2 tablespoons avocado oil until hot. Add the ground pork and salt and use the back of a spatula to press the pork down into a single layer. Cook, undisturbed, until one side is crisp and golden brown, about 4 minutes. Continue to cook, breaking up the pork with the edge of a spoon, until the pork is cooked through and no longer pink, 2 to 3 more minutes. Using a slotted spoon, transfer the cooked pork to a plate and set aside.

**TO** the same pan, add the cabbage, green onions, and the chili oil with spices and toss until well combined. Cook, tossing often, until the cabbage has softened and has turned bright green, about 3 minutes.

**ADD** the pork and any juices, the rice vinegar, coconut aminos, coconut sugar (if using), and fish sauce. Continue to cook, tossing, until the cabbage and pork are well coated in the sauce, 2 to 3 more minutes.

**REMOVE** from the heat and serve.

### FROM MY KITCHEN TO YOURS

To cut the cabbage, halve the cabbage with a knife vertically through the core. Cut around the core and remove it. With your hands, tear the leaves into 3-inch-wide pieces. I prefer using only the tender leaves, not any with hard stem ends. While you can roughly chop the cabbage with a knife, the hand-torn process ensures that the leaves separate well. A small head of cabbage will yield about 8 cups of 3-inch pieces.

# crunchy baked beef tacos

**MAKES 4 SERVINGS • TOTAL TIME: 50 MINUTES**

2 to 3 tablespoons avocado oil, divided, plus more as needed

¼ cup finely diced white onion (about ½ small onion)

1 pound ground beef (90/10)

1 teaspoon kosher salt

½ teaspoon freshly ground black pepper

½ teaspoon chili powder

½ teaspoon ground cumin

½ teaspoon garlic powder

½ teaspoon onion powder

½ teaspoon dried oregano

One 4-ounce can diced green chiles (hot or mild; I use hot here)

1 tablespoon tomato paste

8 grain-free tortillas (I use Siete brand)

1 cup freshly shredded sharp cheddar cheese (omit and see note for dairy-free and paleo)

FOR SERVING

½ cup finely shredded iceberg lettuce

1 Roma (plum) tomato, seeded and diced small

2 tablespoons finely chopped fresh cilantro

1 lime, cut into wedges

Your favorite hot sauce

*There is nothing quite like a simple beef taco on a busy weeknight. This take on a classic is, in my eyes, the perfect beef taco recipe. While the meat is deliciously seasoned, the real star is the crunchy taco shell. Grain-free tortillas are filled and baked until crisp on the edges, yet still soft in the center. Inspired by one of my favorite drive-thru tacos—shout-out to Jack in the Box—these tacos are just the best!*

PREHEAT the oven to 400°F. Line a sheet pan with parchment paper.

IN a large skillet, heat 1 tablespoon of the avocado oil over medium-high heat. Add the onion and beef and cook, breaking up the meat with the edge of a spoon, until cooked through and no longer pink, about 7 minutes. You want to really break up the meat so it's super small and there are no large chunks. Drain off all but about 2 tablespoons of the fat from the pan.

ADD the salt, black pepper, chili powder, cumin, garlic powder, onion powder, and oregano. Cook, stirring, until the spices are fragrant and incorporated into the meat, 1 to 2 minutes. Add the diced green chiles and tomato paste and toss until well combined with the meat. Remove from the heat, cover, and set aside.

IN a large nonstick skillet, heat ½ teaspoon of the avocado oil over medium-high heat and quickly fry 1 tortilla (about 30 seconds on each side) until it's flexible and easy to fold. Set the tortilla on the prepared sheet pan and scoop about 2 tablespoons of beef onto one side of the tortilla. Sprinkle about 2 tablespoons of cheese (if using) onto the beef, then gently fold the tortilla in half forming a taco. Continue frying, filling, and folding the tacos, adding more oil to the skillet as needed, until you've filled all the tortillas.

TRANSFER the sheet pan to the oven and cook until the tacos are crispy and golden brown on the edges, about 15 minutes.

TO SERVE: Let the tacos cool on the pan until you can handle them. Using your hands, gently open the tacos to fill with the shredded lettuce, diced tomatoes, and chopped cilantro, taking care not to crack the tortilla shell.

SERVE with lime wedges and your favorite hot sauce.

## FROM MY KITCHEN TO YOURS

To keep this recipe dairy-free and paleo, you can either omit the shredded cheese or substitute ½ cup of store-bought cashew queso. Please note that if you do not use any cheese or cashew queso, the tortillas may not hold their shape while cooking. For the method using cashew queso, set a warmed tortilla on the prepared sheet pan and scoop about 2 tablespoons of the beef mixture onto one side of the tortilla. Spread 1 tablespoon of the cashew queso across the other side of the tortilla and gently fold the tortilla in half, forming a taco. Bake as indicated in the recipe.

# sheet pan mini bbq-cheddar meatloaves with sweet potatoes and brussels sprouts

MAKES 4 SERVINGS • TOTAL TIME: 50 MINUTES

## FOR THE VEGGIES

2 cups 1-inch peeled and cubed sweet potato (about 1 large sweet potato)

1 pound Brussels sprouts, tough ends trimmed, halved lengthwise

2 tablespoons extra-virgin olive oil

½ teaspoon garlic powder

1 teaspoon kosher salt

½ teaspoon freshly ground black pepper

## FOR THE MINI MEATLOAVES

1½ pounds lean ground beef (see note)

½ cup minced shallot (about 2 large shallots)

1 teaspoon onion powder

1 teaspoon kosher salt

½ teaspoon freshly ground black pepper

½ teaspoon dried thyme

½ teaspoon garlic powder

1 teaspoon Dijon mustard

1 large egg, whisked

10 tablespoons no-sugar-added barbecue sauce, divided (I use Whole30-approved Noble Made brand)

2 tablespoons almond flour (see note)

½ cup shredded sharp cheddar cheese (omit for dairy-free, paleo, and Whole30)

2 tablespoons finely chopped fresh parsley, plus more for garnish

*I grew up eating my mom's classic meatloaf recipe almost weekly. It's a great way to feed the entire family and leave everyone satisfied. I adapted a traditional recipe to create mini meatloaves that bake quickly and added a store-bought BBQ sauce for extra flavor. With the sweet potatoes and Brussels sprouts, it's a no-fuss sheet pan meal that is sure to be a hit.*

PREHEAT the oven to 400°F. Line a sheet pan with parchment paper.

PREPARE THE VEGGIES: Set the sweet potato and Brussels sprouts on the prepared sheet pan. Drizzle with the oil, season with the garlic powder, salt, and pepper and toss to coat. Bake for 20 minutes.

MEANWHILE, FORM THE MEATLOAVES: In a large bowl, combine the beef, shallot, onion powder, salt, pepper, thyme, garlic powder, mustard, egg, and 2 tablespoons of the barbecue sauce. Using a fork, mix until well combined. Add the almond flour, cheese (if using), and parsley. Mix again until well combined. Using damp hands, divide into 4 equal portions and form into loaves. Set aside.

AFTER 20 minutes, remove the veggies from the oven. Push the vegetables to the edge of the sheet pan, making room in the center for the meatloaves. Place the meatloaves in the center of the sheet pan, leaving about ½ inch of space between the loaves to give them room to cook evenly. Evenly brush the top of each meatloaf with 2 tablespoons of the remaining barbecue sauce.

BAKE until the meatloaves are cooked through and no longer pink in the center, 16 to 18 minutes. The veggies will be golden brown and tender.

## FROM MY KITCHEN TO YOURS

FOR THE GROUND BEEF: It is important to use lean ground beef for this recipe in order for the meatloaves to hold their shape. It is normal for the meatloaves to let out a little bit of liquid when baking, but with a lean ground beef (90/10 or 95/5), you'll have less of it.

FOR THE ALMOND FLOUR: If you are unable to use almond flour, gluten-free panko is a great alternative, but the recipe wouldn't be paleo or Whole30.

# skillet mojo pork tenderloin

**MAKES 4 SERVINGS** • **TOTAL TIME: 45 MINUTES**

## FOR THE MOJO SAUCE

6 tablespoons extra-virgin olive oil

2 tablespoons freshly squeezed orange juice (about ½ orange)

2 tablespoons freshly squeezed lime juice (about 1 lime)

2 tablespoons red wine vinegar

2 cups chopped fresh cilantro leaves (about 2 small bunches)

½ cup chopped fresh mint leaves

5 garlic cloves, roughly chopped

1 teaspoon dried oregano

½ teaspoon ground cumin

½ teaspoon kosher salt

½ teaspoon freshly ground black pepper

## FOR THE PORK SKILLET

2½ teaspoons kosher salt, divided

1 teaspoon freshly ground black pepper, divided

1 teaspoon dried oregano

1 teaspoon paprika

½ teaspoon ground cumin

2 pork tenderloins (about 1 pound each), silver skin removed

2 tablespoons extra-virgin olive oil

2 red bell peppers, sliced into thin strips

1 orange bell pepper, sliced into thin strips

1 medium white onion, halved and thinly sliced

*Mojo, a zippy Cuban sauce packed with herbs and garlic, is often used to marinate slow-roasted pork, but to be honest I'd be happy putting it on just about everything. For a quick and easy skillet dinner, I've opted to sear, then roast pork tenderloin with veggies and serve it drizzled in the beloved mojo sauce. This is great served alone, but also fantastic served with some cilantro-lime rice, black beans, or roasted potatoes for a full, Cuban-inspired meal!*

PREHEAT the oven to 400°F.

MAKE THE MOJO SAUCE: In a blender or using an immersion blender in a wide-mouth jar, blend the mojo sauce ingredients until well combined and almost smooth.

MAKE THE PORK SKILLET: In a small bowl, combine 2 teaspoons of the salt, ½ teaspoon of the black pepper, the oregano, paprika, and cumin. Stir to combine. Evenly sprinkle the spice mixture over the pork tenderloin, then rub it in until the pork is evenly coated.

IN a large deep ovenproof skillet, heat the oil over medium-high heat. Add the pork and sear until golden on both sides, about 2 minutes per side. Transfer to a clean plate and set aside.

TO the skillet, add the bell peppers, onion, remaining ½ teaspoon salt, and remaining ½ teaspoon black pepper. Sauté until tender, about 2 minutes.

NESTLE the pork back into the skillet with the veggies. Drizzle ½ cup of the mojo sauce over the pork and veggies.

TRANSFER to the oven and bake, uncovered, until the pork is cooked through and reaches an internal temperature of 150°F, 20 to 25 minutes.

LET the pork rest on a clean cutting board for 5 to 10 minutes, then slice it into medallions. Serve with the peppers and the remaining mojo sauce.

# easy ground lamb curry

**MAKES 4 SERVINGS** • **TOTAL TIME: 35 MINUTES**

GLUTEN-FREE

GRAIN-FREE

*if modified:*
DAIRY-FREE
PALEO
WHOLE30

2 tablespoons extra-virgin olive oil

1 cup finely diced yellow onion (about ½ onion)

2 garlic cloves, minced

1-inch piece fresh ginger, peeled and finely grated

1 pound ground lamb or beef

1 tablespoon curry powder

1½ teaspoons kosher salt

1 teaspoon garam masala

½ teaspoon ground turmeric

½ teaspoon freshly ground black pepper

¼ teaspoon cayenne pepper

1 tablespoon tomato paste

¾ cup small-diced Roma (plum) tomatoes (about 2 tomatoes)

1 cup medium-diced peeled russet potato (about 1 small potato)

1½ cups low-sodium beef broth

¼ cup frozen peas

⅓ cup plain 2% or whole-milk Greek yogurt (sub unsweetened full-fat coconut milk for dairy-free, paleo, and Whole30)

### FOR SERVING

Prepared steamed rice (sub cauliflower rice for Whole30, paleo, and grain-free)

Roughly chopped fresh cilantro, for garnish

*If you're looking for a comforting and flavorful meal in under 40 minutes, this recipe will do the trick! Ground lamb is used to make a quick and easy Indian-inspired curry that is so tasty and a complete win with my whole family. The combination of dried spices adds a depth of flavor that is finished with creamy and tangy Greek yogurt for a simple dish with robust flavor.*

IN a large skillet, heat the oil over medium-high heat. Add the onion, garlic, and ginger and sauté until tender, about 3 minutes.

ADD the ground lamb and cook, breaking up the meat with the edge of a spoon, until browned and cooked through, about 7 minutes. Drain the excess fat and return the lamb to the pan. Reduce the heat to medium.

ADD the curry powder, salt, garam masala, turmeric, black pepper, and cayenne. Cook, stirring until the spices are fragrant, about 2 minutes.

STIR in the tomato paste until well combined. Stir in the tomatoes, potato, and broth and bring to a rapid simmer. Reduce the heat to a light simmer, cover, and cook until the potatoes are tender, about 10 minutes.

UNCOVER and reduce the heat to low. Stir in the peas and yogurt (or coconut milk) and continue cooking until the peas are tender and bright green, about 3 minutes.

TO SERVE: Spoon next to the prepared rice and garnish with cilantro.

# beef enchilada-stuffed acorn squash

**MAKES 4 SERVINGS** • **TOTAL TIME: 50 MINUTES**

## FOR THE SQUASH

2 medium acorn squashes (about 1 pound each), halved through the stem

1 tablespoon extra-virgin olive oil

½ teaspoon kosher salt

## FOR THE BEEF FILLING

2 tablespoons extra-virgin olive oil

½ cup small-diced yellow onion (about ½ small onion)

1 pound ground beef (85/15)

1 tablespoon chili powder

1 teaspoon kosher salt

1 teaspoon ground cumin

1 teaspoon garlic powder

½ teaspoon freshly ground black pepper

½ teaspoon smoked paprika

½ teaspoon dried oregano

¼ teaspoon cayenne pepper, optional

2 tablespoons tomato paste

1 cup low-sodium beef broth, divided

One 4-ounce can mild diced green chiles

2 teaspoons tapioca flour

2 tablespoons freshly squeezed lime juice (about 1 lime)

1 cup shredded Monterey Jack cheese (omit for dairy-free, paleo, and Whole30)

½ jalapeño, thinly sliced, optional

## OPTIONAL FOR SERVING

Pico de gallo or salsa

Fresh cilantro leaves, chopped

1 lime, cut into wedges

*This is one of my favorite recipes to make on repeat when acorn squash is in season! The subtly sweet flavor of the squash in combination with the savory beef enchilada filling is a match made in heaven.*

**PREHEAT** the oven to 425°F.

**PREPARE THE SQUASH:** Using a sharp spoon, scoop out the seeds and discard. Place the squash cut side up in a 9 × 13-inch baking dish. Brush the flesh of the squash with the oil and season evenly with the salt. Flip the squash so it is cut side down and bake until the squash is fork-tender, about 30 minutes.

**MEANWHILE, MAKE THE BEEF FILLING:** In a large deep nonstick skillet, heat the oil over medium-high heat. Add the onion and sauté until it begins to soften, about 2 minutes. Add the beef and cook, breaking up the meat with the edge of a spoon, until browned and cooked through, 5 to 7 minutes. If needed, drain off the excess fat and transfer the beef back to the pan.

**REDUCE** the heat to medium and add the chili powder, salt, cumin, garlic powder, black pepper, smoked paprika, oregano, and cayenne (if using) and cook, stirring, until the spices are fragrant, about 2 minutes.

**STIR** in the tomato paste until well combined. Add ½ cup of the broth and the green chiles and stir until well combined.

**IN** a small bowl, whisk together the remaining ½ cup broth and the tapioca flour. Add to the beef mixture and stir to combine. Add the lime juice and stir to combine once more. Cover and keep warm while the squash finishes roasting.

**TO ASSEMBLE THE SQUASH,** carefully flip the squash so it is cut side up. Evenly divide the filling among the four squash boats; it will overflow slightly. Evenly divide the shredded cheese (if using) over the filling. Top with the sliced jalapeños (if using).

**BAKE** until the cheese is melted, about 5 minutes. If not using cheese, do not return to the oven.

**IF** desired, serve the squash with pico de gallo, cilantro, and lime wedges.

# sichuan-inspired beef stir-fry

MAKES 4 SERVINGS  •  TOTAL TIME: 45 MINUTES

1½ pounds sirloin steak, trimmed of any fat and thinly sliced against the grain (see note)

3 tablespoons avocado oil, divided

1 tablespoon tapioca flour

1 teaspoon kosher salt

½ teaspoon garlic powder

½ teaspoon freshly ground black pepper

1 teaspoon toasted sesame oil

¼ teaspoon crushed red pepper flakes, plus more for serving (optional)

¼ teaspoon freshly crushed Sichuan peppercorns (I place the peppercorns in a bag and crush using the back of a spoon)

1-inch piece fresh ginger, peeled and finely grated

2 cups matchstick-cut green onions (about 5 green onions)

2 cups matchstick-cut carrots (about 1 medium carrot)

2 cups matchstick-cut celery (about 2 stalks)

¼ cup coconut aminos

1 tablespoon rice vinegar

1 teaspoon fish sauce (I use Red Boat brand)

Prepared steamed rice (sub cauliflower rice for Whole30, paleo, and grain-free), optional for serving

2 teaspoons toasted sesame seeds, for garnish

*This beef stir-fry has been a favorite of mine for years. Thin beef strips are stir-fried with thin-cut vegetables and tossed in a savory, spicy sauce. And while this recipe does have a kick, you can adjust the red pepper flakes to your heat preference. The addition of the Sichuan peppercorns gives a lovely, mouth-tingling effect to really take the dish to the next level! It does take extra time to cut the vegetables, but the end result is totally worth the work—plus, you can always cut the veggies ahead of time to make assembly simpler.*

PLACE the sliced steak in a large bowl and drizzle with 1 tablespoon of the avocado oil. Sprinkle with the tapioca flour, salt, garlic powder, and black pepper and toss to coat evenly.

IN a large nonstick skillet, heat the remaining 2 tablespoons avocado oil and the sesame oil over medium-high heat. When the oil is hot but not yet smoking, working in batches so as not to overcrowd the skillet, carefully add the beef in a single layer. Cook until the beef is golden brown on both sides, 2 to 3 minutes per side. Transfer the cooked beef to a clean plate.

REDUCE the heat to medium and add the pepper flakes, Sichuan peppercorns, ginger, green onions, carrots, and celery and sauté, stirring often, until the veggies are tender, about 4 minutes.

STIR in the coconut aminos, rice vinegar, and fish sauce and bring to a simmer. Return the seared beef and any juices to the skillet and cook, stirring occasionally, until the sauce has thickened, 2 to 3 minutes.

SERVE alone or over prepared rice. Garnish with toasted sesame seeds and additional pepper flakes, if using.

## FROM MY KITCHEN TO YOURS

To slice the meat very thinly, set the steak in the freezer for about 15 minutes, then thinly slice the steak against the grain into about ¼-inch-wide strips. Cut the longer strips of meat in half so all pieces are a uniform size, 2 to 3 inches long.

170    ROASTED FISH AND WHITE BEAN PUTTANESCA

173    BAKED SALMON SUSHI BOWLS WITH SPICY MAYO

174    CREAMY CAJUN FISH

176    CRUNCHY BLACKENED SALMON TACOS WITH SERRANO SLAW

178    HARISSA FISH EN PAPILLOTE

181    TOM YUM–INSPIRED SHRIMP STIR-FRY

182    MEDITERRANEAN SALMON BURGERS WITH CUCUMBER-FETA SALAD

185    SAFFRON-SPICED SHRIMP SKILLET

186    SHEET PAN COCONUT-CRUSTED FISH WITH HONEY-CHILI DRIZZLE

189    JALAPEÑO TUNA CAKE MELTS

190    BLACKENED SHEET PAN SALMON WITH JALAPEÑO TARTAR SAUCE

193    BANG BANG SHRIMP LETTUCE WRAPS

194    RED SNAPPER VERACRUZANA

seafood

# roasted fish and white bean puttanesca

**MAKES 4 SERVINGS • TOTAL TIME: 30 MINUTES**

Two 15-ounce cans cannellini beans, drained and rinsed

One 13.8-ounce carton chopped tomatoes (I use Pomì brand)

½ cup halved and thinly sliced shallot (about 1 large shallot)

2 garlic cloves, thinly sliced

¾ cup pitted kalamata olives, torn in half

2 tablespoons capers, drained

2 tablespoons finely chopped fresh parsley, plus more for serving (optional)

1 tablespoon finely chopped fresh oregano leaves

3 tablespoons extra-virgin olive oil, divided

½ teaspoon crushed red pepper flakes

1 teaspoon kosher salt, divided

1 teaspoon freshly ground black pepper, divided

1 small lemon, thinly sliced into rounds, seeds removed

4 skinless halibut, cod, or other flaky white fish fillets (6 ounces each)

*Puttanesca is the OG pantry-based pasta dish. Traditionally made with pasta, tomatoes, capers, and olives, it's a use-what-you-have weeknight winner. In place of the pasta, I've opted instead to use one of my favorite pantry ingredients of all time: cannellini beans. The velvety-soft yet hearty beans are the perfect vehicle to soak up the fantastic puttanesca flavors in this meal. Topped off with a flaky white fish and made in one dish, this is the perfect weeknight dinner yet also elegant enough to serve at a dinner party.*

PREHEAT the oven to 375°F.

IN a 9 × 13-inch baking dish or a 6 × 9-inch 1-quart oval roasting pan, combine the beans, tomatoes, shallot, garlic, olives, capers, parsley, oregano, 2 tablespoons of the oil, the pepper flakes, and ½ teaspoon each of the salt and black pepper. Gently toss until well combined. Nestle in the lemon slices, arranging them around the pan.

PLACE the fish fillets on top of the white bean mixture and drizzle with the remaining 1 tablespoon oil. Sprinkle the fillets with the remaining ½ teaspoon each of the salt and black pepper.

ROAST until the fish is cooked through and flakes easily when pressed with a fork, 18 to 20 minutes.

PLATE the fish and spoon the white bean puttanesca over and around the fillet. Garnish with fresh parsley, if desired.

# baked salmon sushi bowls with spicy mayo

MAKES 4 SERVINGS • TOTAL TIME: 45 MINUTES

GLUTEN-FREE
DAIRY-FREE
*if modified:*
PALEO
WHOLE30

## FOR THE SALMON

2 pounds center-cut salmon, skin and pin bones removed

1 tablespoon avocado oil

½ cup coconut aminos

2 tablespoons freshly squeezed lime juice (about 1 lime)

2 garlic cloves, minced

1-inch piece fresh ginger, peeled and finely grated

1 teaspoon toasted sesame oil

1 teaspoon kosher salt

½ teaspoon ground white pepper

## FOR THE SPICY MAYO

¼ cup Homemade Mayo (page 7)

½ teaspoon toasted sesame oil

2 tablespoons no-sugar-added sriracha (I use Yellowbird brand)

1 tablespoon rice vinegar

2 garlic cloves, minced

## FOR THE BOWLS

2 cups prepared brown rice (sub cauliflower rice for paleo and Whole30)

1 avocado, sliced

2 Persian (mini) cucumbers, thinly sliced on the diagonal

2 green onions, thinly sliced on the diagonal

One 4.5-gram package premium roasted seaweed or nori wraps, thinly sliced

1 tablespoon toasted sesame seeds

1 lime, cut into wedges

*Slow-roasted salmon rests on a pillowy mound of steamed brown rice along with crisp cucumber slices, creamy avocado, and salty nori in this healthy weeknight sushi bowl recipe. Finished off with simple spicy mayo, this is definitely one of my family's favorite weeknight dinners. Set it up on the dinner table for a build-your-own bowl night and take the time to connect around the table with your loved ones!*

PREHEAT the oven to 325°F.

BAKE THE SALMON: Pat the salmon dry and place it in a medium baking dish (I use a 2½-quart oval baking dish). In a small bowl, whisk together the avocado oil, coconut aminos, lime juice, garlic, ginger, and sesame oil until well combined. Pour over the salmon to coat it evenly. Sprinkle the salmon with the salt and white pepper.

BAKE for 15 minutes. Baste the salmon by spooning the sauce over the fillet. Continue baking until the salmon flakes easily with a fork, about 15 more minutes.

MAKE THE SPICY MAYO: In a small bowl, whisk together the spicy mayo ingredients. Set aside.

PREPARE THE BOWLS: Flake the salmon into large pieces with a fork. Spoon the rice into four bowls, top with the salmon, and spoon a bit of the cooking sauce on top. Garnish the bowls as desired with avocado, cucumber, green onions, and nori strips. Drizzle with the spicy mayo, sprinkle with the toasted sesame seeds, and serve with a lime wedge.

# creamy cajun fish

**MAKES 4 SERVINGS** • **TOTAL TIME: 30 MINUTES**

1½ teaspoons paprika

1 teaspoon dried oregano

1 teaspoon dried rosemary

1 teaspoon dried thyme

¼ teaspoon cayenne pepper, or more to taste

4 skinless halibut, cod, salmon (see note), or other flaky fish fillets (6 ounces each)

1 teaspoon kosher salt

½ teaspoon freshly ground black pepper

2 tablespoons extra-virgin olive oil, plus more as needed

2 garlic cloves, minced

½ cup finely diced shallot (about 1 large shallot)

1 red bell pepper, sliced into ¼-inch-wide strips

2 teaspoons Dijon mustard

1 cup unsweetened full-fat coconut milk

½ cup low-sodium seafood stock or chicken broth

2 tablespoons freshly squeezed lemon juice (about 1 lemon)

2 cups baby spinach

2 tablespoons finely chopped fresh parsley leaves

*This creamy, Cajun-inspired fish is an incredibly delicious and easy 30-minute meal. Blackened fish and sautéed bell peppers simmer in a lush and absolutely irresistible creamy Cajun-seasoned sauce. It's a comforting dinner that you can serve over pasta, rice, mashed potatoes, or on its own. The touch of cayenne gives it a little heat, but my family doesn't find it spicy at all and my kiddos eat it as is. If you want a spicier dish, I suggest adding a bit more cayenne for a kick!*

IN a small bowl, mix the paprika, oregano, rosemary, thyme, and cayenne.

PAT the fish very dry with a paper towel. Season both sides with the salt, black pepper, and 3 teaspoons of the seasoning mixture. Set the rest of the seasoning mixture aside for sautéing the veggies.

IN a large deep nonstick skillet, heat the oil over medium-high heat. Carefully add the fish and sear until golden brown, about 2 minutes per side. The fish doesn't need to be fully cooked through, as it will finish cooking in the sauce. Transfer the browned fish to a clean plate and set aside.

REDUCE the heat to medium and add more oil to the skillet if it seems dry. Add the garlic, shallot, and bell pepper and cook, stirring occasionally, until the bell pepper is tender, about 3 minutes.

ADD the reserved seasoning mixture and cook, stirring, toasting the spices until fragrant, about 1 minute.

ADD the mustard, coconut milk, stock, and lemon juice and stir to combine. Bring the sauce to a simmer and cook, stirring, until the sauce begins to thicken a bit, about 3 minutes.

STIR in the spinach until just wilted. Reduce the heat to a light simmer and nestle the fish back into the sauce. Continue to cook, uncovered, until the fish is just cooked through and flakes easily with a fork, 2 to 3 more minutes.

GARNISH with parsley.

### FROM MY KITCHEN TO YOURS

While any flaky fish works with this recipe, I like to use halibut, cod, or salmon. Just note that with salmon, depending on the thickness of the fillets, you may need to increase the cooking time by 2 to 3 more minutes while the fillets simmer in the sauce.

# crunchy blackened salmon tacos with serrano slaw

**MAKES 4 SERVINGS** • **TOTAL TIME: 35 MINUTES**

## FOR THE SLAW

2 cups very finely shredded red cabbage

2 cups very finely shredded green cabbage

1 tablespoon finely chopped fresh oregano leaves or 1 teaspoon dried

1 serrano pepper, very thinly sliced into rounds

¼ cup extra-virgin olive oil

2 tablespoons freshly squeezed lime juice (about 1 lime)

2 tablespoons freshly squeezed lemon juice (about 1 lemon)

¼ teaspoon kosher salt

¼ teaspoon freshly ground black pepper

## FOR THE DRIZZLE

3 tablespoons Homemade Mayo (page 7)

1 tablespoon freshly squeezed lime juice (about ½ lime)

2 teaspoons of your favorite hot sauce (I use El Yucateco), plus more for serving

*Not to be dramatic, but these tacos are kind of life-changing. First off, don't be intimidated by the lengthy ingredient list—many of the ingredients are spices you likely already have in your pantry! You'll pack the seasoned salmon into tortillas with a tangy serrano slaw, and drizzle with a quick creamy sauce for a completely showstopping meal.*

**MAKE THE SLAW:** In a large bowl, combine the slaw ingredients. Toss until well combined. Set aside to let the flavors meld while you prepare the rest of the tacos.

**MAKE THE DRIZZLE:** In a small bowl, whisk together the drizzle ingredients until smooth.

**COOK THE SALMON:** Set up a dredging station with two shallow bowls: In one bowl, mix together the thyme, paprika, garlic powder, cayenne (if using), salt, black pepper, and panko and mix well. In a second bowl, whisk the egg with 1 teaspoon water.

**WORKING** with one strip at a time, dip the salmon into the egg wash and shake off the excess. Then roll the salmon in the panko mixture until evenly coated. Continue to bread all the salmon and set aside.

**LINE** a plate with paper towels. In a large nonstick skillet, heat the oil over medium heat until shimmering. Working in batches if necessary, so as not to overcrowd the pan, gently add the breaded salmon to the hot oil. Cook until golden brown and cooked through, 2 to 3 minutes per side, taking care to turn the salmon very gently. Transfer the cooked salmon to the plate lined with paper towels.

**ASSEMBLE THE TACOS:** One at a time, place the tortillas in a dry (no oil) skillet over medium heat and cook for about 30 seconds on each side. (Alternatively, you can char the tortillas directly over a gas flame for a few seconds using tongs.)

**FOR** each taco, place a small amount of the slaw in a warm tortilla. Top with the blackened salmon and the drizzle and garnish with cilantro. Serve with hot sauce, if desired.

### FOR THE SALMON

1 teaspoon dried thyme

1 teaspoon paprika

1 teaspoon garlic powder

½ teaspoon cayenne pepper, optional

1 teaspoon kosher salt

½ teaspoon freshly ground black pepper

⅓ cup gluten-free panko bread crumbs (I use Aleia's brand)

1 large egg

1 pound center-cut salmon, skin and pin bones removed, cut into 1-inch-wide and 2-inch-long strips

¼ cup extra-virgin olive oil

### FOR THE TACOS

8 grain-free tortillas (I use Siete brand)

¼ cup finely chopped fresh cilantro

Hot sauce, optional for serving

# harissa fish en papillote

**MAKES 2 SERVINGS** • **TOTAL TIME: 35 MINUTES**

½ lemon, cut into ¼-inch-thick rounds, seeds removed

6 ounces haricots verts or green beans, trimmed

2 skinless halibut, cod, or other flaky white fish fillets (6 ounces each)

½ teaspoon kosher salt

½ teaspoon freshly ground black pepper

3 tablespoons extra-virgin olive oil

1 teaspoon Dijon mustard

1 tablespoon spicy or mild harissa (I use Mina brand)

½ teaspoon ground coriander

½ teaspoon curry powder

½ teaspoon ground turmeric

¼ cup pitted Castelvetrano olives, torn in half

2 teaspoons roughly chopped fresh oregano leaves

1 cup cooked quinoa, for serving (omit for paleo, Whole30, and grain-free)

*Fish en papillote—don't you feel fancy just saying it? Despite its elegant name, this method of baking fish in parchment paper packets is one of the easiest, most foolproof ways there is. In this recipe, flaky white fish is paired with lemon, harissa, Dijon mustard, a blend of warm seasonings, olives, and fresh oregano. As the fish bakes, it steams in lemon and harissa, resulting in an incredibly tender and delicious dinner.*

PREHEAT the oven to 400°F.

LAY out two 12 × 14-inch pieces of parchment paper on a flat surface. Evenly divide the lemon rounds and place them in the center of each piece of parchment, then divide the green beans and place them on the lemon slices. Place a fish fillet on each arrangement of green beans. Season the fillets with the salt and pepper.

IN a small bowl, whisk together the oil, mustard, harissa, coriander, curry powder, and turmeric until well combined. Drizzle the sauce evenly over the fish fillets, then top them with the olives and oregano.

TO close the packets, bring up the two short ends to meet in the middle over the fish, then fold the ends down together to make a rectangle. Fold each of the open ends toward the fish, rolling them up much as you would roll the top of a brown paper lunch bag. You want to create an enclosed package so that no liquids can escape.

PLACE the parcels on a sheet pan and place the pan in the oven. Roast until the fish is cooked through and flakes easily with a fork, about 18 minutes.

LET the packets rest for at least 3 minutes before carefully opening them. Serve with the cooked quinoa (if using).

# tom yum-inspired shrimp stir-fry

MAKES 4 SERVINGS • TOTAL TIME: 30 MINUTES

GLUTEN-FREE

DAIRY-FREE

PALEO

GRAIN-FREE

*if modified:*
WHOLE30

1 pound peeled and deveined shrimp (31/40 count, tail optional)

3 to 4 tablespoons avocado oil, divided, plus more if needed

2 tablespoons tapioca flour

1 tablespoon coconut sugar (omit for Whole30)

1 teaspoon ground coriander

1 teaspoon kosher salt

½ teaspoon freshly ground black pepper

1 cup halved and thinly sliced white onion (about 1 small onion)

2 cups quartered baby bella mushrooms

2 cups cherry tomatoes

2 tablespoons minced lemongrass (about 2 lemongrass stalks, tender white inner bulb only, see note on page 149)

2 garlic cloves, thinly sliced

1 to 3 Thai chiles (1 for mild, 3 for hot), thinly sliced

1-inch piece fresh ginger, peeled and finely grated

Grated zest of ½ lime

2 tablespoons freshly squeezed lime juice (about 1 lime)

1 tablespoon fish sauce (I use Red Boat brand)

2 tablespoons coconut aminos

1 cup fresh cilantro leaves and tender stems, roughly chopped

Prepared steamed rice (sub cauliflower rice for Whole30, paleo, and grain-free), optional for serving

*This shrimp stir-fry is a unique twist on the flavors of the traditional Thai tom yum soup. The craveable, sweet, spicy, and tangy flavors within this simple stir-fry are absolutely irresistible. You'll definitely want to have all of your ingredients prepped, chopped, and ready to go ahead of time as the shrimp cooks quickly!*

PAT the shrimp dry with a paper towel and place them in a large bowl. Add 1 tablespoon of the avocado oil, the tapioca flour, coconut sugar (if using), ground coriander, salt, and pepper and toss until well combined.

IN a large deep nonstick skillet, heat the remaining 2 tablespoons oil over medium-high heat. Add the shrimp and spread it in a single layer across the bottom of the skillet. Cook, undisturbed, until a light golden-brown crust has formed on one side, 2 to 3 minutes. Toss the shrimp and continue to cook until the shrimp are pink and opaque, about 2 more minutes. Using a slotted spoon, transfer the cooked shrimp to a plate and set aside.

TO the same skillet, add the onion and mushrooms. If the skillet seems dry, add another tablespoon of avocado oil. Cook, stirring often, until the onion and mushrooms are slightly tender, 3 to 4 minutes.

ADD the tomatoes, lemongrass, garlic, Thai chiles, and ginger and cook, stirring, until fragrant, about 1 minute.

REDUCE the heat to medium-low and return the shrimp and any of its juices to the skillet. Add the lime zest, lime juice, fish sauce, and coconut aminos. Toss until the shrimp is well coated and the sauce has thickened a bit, about 2 more minutes.

REMOVE from the heat and stir in the cilantro. If desired, serve with prepared rice.

# mediterranean salmon burgers with cucumber-feta salad

**MAKES 6 SERVINGS** • **TOTAL TIME: 40 MINUTES**

## FOR THE CUCUMBER SALAD

4 cups thinly sliced Persian (mini) cucumber (about 4 cucumbers)

1 cup halved and thinly sliced red onion (about ½ medium onion)

½ cup finely chopped fresh mint leaves

¾ cup pitted and torn kalamata olives

¼ cup extra-virgin olive oil

¼ cup freshly squeezed lemon juice (about 2 lemons)

½ teaspoon freshly ground black pepper

¾ cup crumbled feta cheese (omit for dairy-free, paleo, and Whole30)

## FOR THE SALMON BURGERS

¼ cup loosely packed fresh dill fronds

½ cup loosely packed fresh parsley leaves

2 garlic cloves, peeled

1 teaspoon dried oregano

¼ teaspoon crushed red pepper flakes

2 pounds center-cut salmon, skin and pin bones removed

1 large egg yolk

1 teaspoon kosher salt

½ teaspoon freshly ground black pepper

2 tablespoons tapioca flour

Grated zest of ½ lemon

2 tablespoons extra-virgin olive oil

## FOR SERVING

6 cups baby arugula

*In the Snodgrass household, salmon is a staple. Because we have it so often, I like to think of fun new ways to enjoy the protein, and salmon burgers are definitely one of my favorite ways to shake things up. If you've never made salmon burgers, don't be intimidated. You simply pulse fresh salmon in a food processor. The salmon is then infused with bright Mediterranean flavors, seared on the stovetop, and topped with a cool, fresh cucumber salad. It makes for a beautiful weeknight dinner!*

**MAKE THE CUCUMBER SALAD:** In a medium bowl, combine the cucumbers, onion, mint, olives, oil, lemon juice, and black pepper. Toss until well combined. Add the feta (if using) and gently toss once more. Set aside in the fridge until ready to serve.

**MAKE THE SALMON BURGERS:** In a food processor, combine the dill, parsley, garlic, oregano, and pepper flakes and pulse until roughly chopped.

**PAT** the salmon dry and cut it into 2-inch cubes. Working in batches as needed, add the salmon to the food processor with the herbs and pulse until the mixture is almost the texture of ground beef. You don't want it overprocessed. Transfer to a medium bowl.

**TO** the salmon mixture, add the egg yolk, salt, black pepper, tapioca flour, and lemon zest. Stir to combine.

**DIVIDE** the salmon mixture into 6 equal portions (about a heaping ½ cup each) and shape into patties. Place them on a large plate or sheet pan.

**LINE** a plate with paper towels. In a large nonstick skillet, heat the oil over medium heat. Add the salmon burgers, working in batches as needed, and cook until each side is golden brown and the salmon is cooked through, 3 to 4 minutes per side. Transfer to the plate lined with paper towels.

**TO SERVE:** Arrange 1 cup of arugula on each plate. Lay a salmon burger on the greens and top with some cucumber salad.

# saffron-spiced shrimp skillet

**MAKES 4 SERVINGS** • **TOTAL TIME: 35 MINUTES**

## FOR THE SHRIMP

1 pound peeled and deveined medium shrimp (31/35 count, tail optional)

2 tablespoons extra-virgin olive oil

½ teaspoon kosher salt

¼ teaspoon freshly ground black pepper

¼ teaspoon smoked paprika

¼ teaspoon cayenne pepper

Grated zest of ½ lemon

## FOR THE RICE

1 teaspoon saffron threads

½ cup dry white wine

2 tablespoons extra-virgin olive oil

1 cup halved and thinly sliced yellow onion (about 1 small onion)

1 red bell pepper, thinly sliced

3 garlic cloves, minced

1 teaspoon kosher salt

½ teaspoon freshly ground black pepper

1 teaspoon ground turmeric

½ teaspoon ground cumin

1 cup basmati rice, rinsed until the water runs clear

1¼ cups low-sodium chicken broth, divided

½ cup pitted Castelvetrano olives, torn in half

1 tablespoon chopped fresh parsley

## FOR SERVING

Chopped fresh parsley, for garnish

1 lemon, cut into wedges

*This easy shrimp and rice skillet is the perfect complete meal that is packed with fabulous flavor. Loosely inspired by the flavors of paella, this rice dish is filled with aromatics like onion, garlic, saffron, cumin, and turmeric for an elegant and beautiful dinner. Here, parcooked rice is topped off with shrimp and finished in the oven so the shrimp can roast. It's beautiful in every way, and a total crowd-pleaser for the family!*

PREHEAT the oven to 375°F.

PREPARE THE SHRIMP: In a large bowl, combine the shrimp, oil, salt, black pepper, smoked paprika, cayenne, and lemon zest and toss until well combined. Set aside while you start the rice.

PREPARE THE RICE: In a small bowl, stir together the saffron and white wine. Set aside and allow the saffron to bloom.

IN a large deep ovenproof skillet with a fitted lid, heat the oil over medium heat until shimmering. Add the onion, bell pepper, garlic, salt, and black pepper and cook, stirring, until the bell pepper and onions are slightly tender, about 3 minutes.

ADD the turmeric, cumin, and rice to the skillet and gently toss to toast, about 1 minute. Stir in the saffron-wine mixture, 1 cup of the broth, and the olives and bring to a boil. Reduce to a light simmer over low heat, cover, and cook for 15 minutes.

WHEN the rice has been cooking for 15 minutes, remove it from the heat and fluff with a fork (it won't be fully cooked). Pour the remaining ¼ cup broth into the rice and add the parsley. Stir to combine. Add the shrimp in a single layer on top of the rice and transfer to the oven. Cook, uncovered, until the shrimp are just pink and cooked through, 8 to 10 minutes. Remove from the oven.

TO SERVE: Garnish with parsley and serve with lemon wedges.

# sheet pan coconut-crusted fish with honey-chili drizzle

MAKES 4 SERVINGS  •  TOTAL TIME: 25 MINUTES

## FOR THE SHEET PAN

2 large broccolini bunches

4 tablespoons avocado oil, divided

¾ teaspoon kosher salt, divided

¼ teaspoon freshly ground black pepper

4 skinless halibut, cod, or other flaky white fish fillets (6 ounces each)

1 tablespoon Dijon mustard

3 tablespoons gluten-free panko bread crumbs (I use Aleia's brand)

3 tablespoons unsweetened shredded coconut

½ teaspoon paprika

## FOR THE HONEY-CHILI DRIZZLE

3 tablespoons honey

1 tablespoon no-sugar-added sriracha (I use Yellowbird brand)

1 teaspoon Dijon mustard

1 teaspoon apple cider vinegar

*The flavors of this coconut-crusted fish transport me right back to Kauai—our go-to summer family vacation destination. When traveling there, we always dine at Tahiti Nui in Hanalei, where Clayton and I sip their famous mai tais and we all eat endless amounts of their coconut-crusted shrimp. Inspired by their shrimp dish, this sheet pan dinner will be on the table in no time, and the flavors will transport you to someplace magical.*

PREHEAT the oven to 400°F. Line a large sheet pan with parchment paper.

TRIM 2 inches off the ends of the broccolini stems and cut any thick stalks in half lengthwise. Place the broccolini on the prepared sheet pan and toss with 2 tablespoons of the avocado oil, ¼ teaspoon of the salt, and the black pepper. Toss until well coated. Push the broccolini to each side of the sheet pan, leaving space in the center for the fish.

PLACE the fish fillets in the center of the sheet pan and pat dry. Divide the Dijon on the tops of the fillets and brush to evenly coat the tops.

IN a small bowl, combine the panko, shredded coconut, paprika, remaining ½ teaspoon salt, and remaining 2 tablespoons avocado oil. Stir until well combined.

EVENLY distribute the panko mixture over the fillets, pressing down and spreading it so that it evenly coats the top of each fillet.

TRANSFER to the oven and bake until the fish is cooked through and flakes easily with a fork and the broccolini is tender, 15 to 18 minutes, tossing the broccolini halfway through.

MEANWHILE, MAKE THE HONEY-CHILI DRIZZLE: In a small bowl, whisk together the honey-chili drizzle ingredients until well combined. Set aside.

WHEN the fish is cooked through, divide among four plates with the broccolini. Top the fish and broccolini with the honey-chili drizzle.

# jalapeño tuna cake melts

**MAKES 4 SERVINGS • TOTAL TIME: 25 MINUTES**

Two 5-ounce cans no-salt-added water-packed tuna, drained

1 large egg, whisked

2 garlic cloves, minced

¼ cup finely diced red onion (about ¼ small onion)

¼ cup minced pickled jalapeños

2 tablespoons finely chopped fresh dill, plus more fronds for garnish

2 tablespoons Homemade Mayo (page 7)

1 teaspoon Dijon mustard

¼ cup finely diced celery (about ½ stalk)

Grated zest of ½ lemon

½ teaspoon kosher salt

½ teaspoon freshly ground black pepper

¼ cup gluten-free panko bread crumbs (I use Aleia's brand)

1 tablespoon tapioca flour

2 tablespoons extra-virgin olive oil

8 thin slices Roma (plum) tomatoes (about 2 tomatoes)

4 slices provolone cheese

1 lemon, cut into wedges

*I know it gets a bad rap, but I'm pushing for canned tuna justice! It's a great source of protein, versatile for cooking, and super convenient to have on hand when you need to shop your pantry instead of the store. This recipe is a fun and lower-carb twist on a classic tuna melt. Delicious tuna cakes are seared on the stovetop, topped with tomatoes and provolone cheese, and finished under the broiler for the perfect melt. Served over a bed of arugula or with a side of roasted asparagus, it's a recipe that I love to turn to on a busy night!*

PLACE the drained tuna in a large bowl and use a fork to gently break up the bigger chunks. Add the egg, garlic, onion, jalapeños, dill, mayo, mustard, celery, lemon zest, salt, black pepper, panko, and tapioca flour. Stir to combine.

IN a large broiler-safe skillet, heat the oil over medium heat. Divide the tuna mixture into 4 equal portions (about ⅓ packed cup each) and form into patties. When the oil is hot, use a spatula to carefully lay the cakes into the oil. Fry until golden brown on one side, about 3 minutes. Carefully flip the tuna cakes and immediately remove the skillet from the heat.

TURN the oven to broil. If you don't have a broiler, turn your oven to its hottest setting. Lay 2 slices of tomato on each tuna cake and top each with a slice of cheese. Place under the broiler for about 2 minutes to melt the cheese, watching carefully so as not to burn it.

GARNISH the broiled tuna cakes with dill fronds. Serve with lemon wedges.

# blackened sheet pan salmon with jalapeño tartar sauce

**MAKES 4 SERVINGS** • **TOTAL TIME: 50 MINUTES**

## FOR THE SALMON AND VEGGIES

1 tablespoon coconut sugar

2 teaspoons kosher salt

1 teaspoon freshly ground black pepper

1 teaspoon chipotle chile powder

1 teaspoon dried oregano

2 red bell peppers, sliced into ¼-inch-wide strips

1 small yellow onion, halved and thinly sliced

2 small unpeeled sweet potatoes, halved lengthwise and sliced into half-moons

5 tablespoons extra-virgin olive oil, divided

4 skin-on salmon fillets, pin bones removed (6 ounces each)

## FOR THE JALAPEÑO TARTAR SAUCE

½ cup plain 2% or whole-milk Greek yogurt (sub nondairy sour cream for dairy-free and paleo)

2 tablespoons extra-virgin olive oil

2 garlic cloves, peeled

¼ cup fresh cilantro leaves and tender stems, plus more for serving

¼ cup fresh dill fronds, plus more for serving

1 medium jalapeño, seeded and roughly chopped

2 tablespoons freshly squeezed lemon juice (about 1 lemon)

1 teaspoon distilled white vinegar

¼ teaspoon kosher salt

¼ teaspoon freshly ground black pepper

2 tablespoons capers, drained and roughly chopped

*While the ingredient list may look a little lengthy, take note that most of the ingredients are pantry staples! Aside from the veggies, salmon, and fresh herbs, you likely have most of the ingredients already on hand. It makes this recipe a total breeze to prepare, and boy, is the flavor in this one absolutely incredible. It's great as is, but also wonderful over cooked quinoa or brown rice if desired.*

PREHEAT the oven to 425°F. Line a large sheet pan with parchment paper.

PREPARE THE SALMON AND VEGGIES: In a small bowl, mix the coconut sugar, salt, black pepper, chipotle powder, and oregano.

ARRANGE the bell peppers, onion, and sweet potatoes on the prepared sheet pan. Drizzle with 3 tablespoons of the oil and sprinkle with 2 teaspoons of the seasoning mixture and toss until evenly coated. Spread the veggies into a single layer on the sheet pan.

TRANSFER to the oven and roast until the bell pepper is tender and the sweet potatoes begin to develop a golden edge, about 25 minutes.

REMOVE from the oven and toss the vegetables. Push the vegetables to the edges of the sheet pan, making space in the center for the salmon. Pat the salmon fillets dry with a paper towel and place them in the center of the sheet pan. Stir the remaining 2 tablespoons oil into the remaining seasoning mixture to create a paste-like consistency. Divide the mixture evenly among the tops of the salmon fillets, about 2 teaspoons per fillet. Gently brush the mixture to evenly coat the top of each fillet.

ROAST until the salmon is cooked through and flakes easily with a fork, 15 to 18 minutes.

MEANWHILE, MAKE THE JALAPEÑO TARTAR SAUCE: With an immersion blender in a wide-mouth jar, combine the yogurt, oil, garlic, cilantro, dill, jalapeño, lemon juice, vinegar, salt, and black pepper. Blend until smooth. Stir in the capers. Set aside until ready to serve. The sauce can be kept in the fridge for 5 to 7 days.

WHEN the salmon is cooked through, serve with the veggies and jalapeño tartar sauce. Garnish with dill and cilantro, if desired.

# bang bang shrimp lettuce wraps

**MAKES 4 SERVINGS** • **TOTAL TIME: 35 MINUTES**

## FOR THE BANG BANG SAUCE

⅓ cup Homemade Mayo (page 7)

2 tablespoons no-sugar-added sriracha (I use Yellowbird brand)

2 teaspoons rice vinegar

1 teaspoon coconut aminos

1 teaspoon honey (omit for Whole30)

1 garlic clove, minced

1-inch piece fresh ginger, peeled and finely grated

1 teaspoon crushed red pepper flakes

½ teaspoon kosher salt

## FOR THE SHRIMP

1 large egg

¼ cup cassava flour

2 tablespoons tapioca flour

½ teaspoon paprika

1 pound peeled, deveined, and tail-off shrimp (31/40 count)

1 teaspoon kosher salt

½ teaspoon freshly ground black pepper

3 tablespoons avocado oil

## FOR SERVING

1 head butter lettuce, leaves separated, rinsed and patted dry

4 green onions, thinly sliced

1 lime, cut into wedges

*If you've ever dined at a Bonefish Grill, then you've likely enjoyed their very popular Bang Bang Shrimp appetizer. In my at-home rendition, cassava and tapioca flour help create a golden crust on the shrimp, then it's tossed in a spicy, slightly sweet sauce. The shrimp is great in lettuce wraps, but also delicious served with rice.*

LINE a sheet pan with parchment paper. Set aside.

MAKE THE BANG BANG SAUCE: In a small bowl, whisk together the mayo, sriracha, vinegar, coconut aminos, honey (if using), garlic, ginger, pepper flakes, and salt until well combined. Set aside.

COOK THE SHRIMP: Set up a dredging station with two large shallow bowls. In one bowl, whisk the egg well. In the second bowl, combine the cassava flour, tapioca flour, and paprika and mix well.

USING paper towels, pat the shrimp very dry. Season both sides with the salt and black pepper. Using a wet hand and a dry hand, begin to dredge the shrimp. One at a time, dip the shrimp first in the egg mixture with the wet hand and shake off the excess. Then, using your dry hand, dredge the shrimp in the flour mixture to coat it evenly. Shake off any excess flour. As you coat the shrimp, set them on the prepared sheet pan in a single layer so that they do not touch.

LINE a large plate with paper towels. In a large deep nonstick skillet, heat the oil over medium heat. Working in batches as needed to keep the shrimp from touching, lay the shrimp in the pan in a single layer and cook until golden on both sides, 2 to 3 minutes per side. With a slotted spoon, transfer the cooked shrimp to the plate lined with paper towels. Let the shrimp cool slightly, about 3 minutes.

TRANSFER the shrimp to a large bowl and drizzle with the desired amount of bang bang sauce, reserving some for serving. Gently toss until well coated.

TO SERVE: Divide the shrimp among the butter lettuce cups. Garnish with the sliced green onions and lime wedges. Serve the remaining bang bang sauce on the side.

GLUTEN-FREE

DAIRY-FREE

PALEO

GRAIN-FREE

*if modified:*
WHOLE30

# red snapper veracruzana

**MAKES 4 SERVINGS** • **TOTAL TIME: 30 MINUTES**

*Pescado a la veracruzana, or fish in the style of Veracruz, Mexico, is a simple dish that works with almost any type of fish. This dish is filled with some of my all-time favorite ingredients, like capers, olives, garlic, and jalapeño, and I love how it comes together in 30 minutes but is impressive enough when entertaining guests.*

## FOR THE SAUCE

2 tablespoons extra-virgin olive oil

¼ cup seeded and small-diced jalapeño (about 1 medium jalapeño)

½ cup halved and thinly sliced shallot (about 1 large shallot)

½ cup small-diced red bell pepper

2 garlic cloves, minced

½ teaspoon kosher salt, plus more to taste

½ teaspoon freshly ground black pepper, plus more to taste

One 14.5-ounce can crushed tomatoes

½ cup dry white wine (sub fish stock and 1 tablespoon fresh lime juice for Whole30)

1 teaspoon dried oregano

2 tablespoons capers, drained

½ cup halved pitted green olives

¼ teaspoon crushed red pepper flakes, optional

## FOR THE RED SNAPPER

4 skin-on red snapper, redfish, or tilapia fillets (6 to 8 ounces each, 1-inch thick)

1 teaspoon kosher salt

½ teaspoon freshly ground black pepper

2 tablespoons extra-virgin olive oil

## FOR SERVING

2 tablespoons roughly chopped fresh cilantro leaves

1 lime, cut into wedges

**MAKE THE SAUCE:** In a large deep skillet, heat the oil over medium heat. Add the jalapeño, shallot, bell pepper, garlic, salt, and black pepper. Sauté until the veggies are tender, 5 to 7 minutes.

**ADD** the tomatoes, wine (if using), oregano, capers, olives, and pepper flakes (if using) and bring to a simmer. Reduce the heat to a light simmer, stir to combine, and continue to simmer, uncovered, to let the flavors meld while you sear the fish.

**MEANWHILE, PREPARE THE FISH:** Place the fillets on a cutting board and pat dry with a paper towel. Season the flesh side of the fillets with the salt and black pepper.

**IN** a large nonstick skillet, heat the oil over medium-high heat. When the oil is hot but not smoking, place the fillets in the skillet, skin side down. You may need to do this in batches depending on the size of the skillet and fillets. Press the fillets down with the back of a spatula to flatten the fish and ensure the skin is flush with the skillet (it tries to curl).

**COOK** the fish, pressing occasionally with the spatula, until it is nearly opaque and cooked through, with just a small raw area on the very top, 3 to 4 minutes. Using a sturdy spatula, carefully flip the snapper and continue cooking the fish, flesh side down, until it is cooked through and golden brown, about 3 more minutes. Remove the fish and transfer to a large serving dish.

**TO SERVE:** Ladle the sauce over the fillets. Garnish with the cilantro. Serve family-style with lime wedges.

198    CHIPOTLE CAULIFLOWER TOSTADAS

201    TIKKA MASALA–INSPIRED LENTILS

202    ROASTED VEGETABLE PITA WITH HERBY TAHINI

204    SPICY BLISTERED GREEN BEANS

207    SPAGHETTI SQUASH WITH SUN-DRIED TOMATOES
         AND MUSHROOMS

208    RED PEPPER MISO BUDDHA BOWLS

211    SHEET PAN RATATOUILLE WITH CRISPY GNOCCHI

212    PORTOBELLO TACOS WITH SERRANO AVOCADO CREMA

vegetarian

# chipotle cauliflower tostadas

**MAKES 2 SERVINGS • TOTAL TIME: 45 MINUTES**

### FOR THE CAULIFLOWER

4 cups cauliflower, cut into small florets (about 1 small head)

¼ cup avocado oil

1 teaspoon smoked paprika

1 teaspoon chipotle chile powder (or regular chili powder for less heat)

½ teaspoon ground cumin

1 teaspoon kosher salt

### FOR THE TOSTADAS

4 grain-free tortillas (I use Siete brand)

4 teaspoons avocado oil

### FOR THE BEANS

One 15-ounce can black beans, drained and rinsed

¼ cup low-sodium vegetable broth

¼ cup salsa verde

2 tablespoons freshly squeezed lime juice (about 1 lime)

### FOR SERVING

1 large avocado, thinly sliced

1 cup baby arugula

1 lime, cut into wedges

### OPTIONAL GARNISHES

Salsa verde

Cilantro

Halved and thinly sliced red onion

Thinly sliced jalapeño

*This simple meatless meal is one of my absolute favorites. Cauliflower florets are tossed in a lovely spice mixture, roasted until golden brown, and served on a crisp tortilla—aka tostada—topped with a swipe of mashed black beans and other delicious toppings like avocado, arugula, and red onions to finish it all off. The chipotle powder in the spice mixture makes these quite spicy. If you're sensitive to heat, swap in regular chili powder, which is much milder.*

PREHEAT the oven to 375°F. Line two large sheet pans with parchment paper.

ROAST THE CAULIFLOWER: Place the cauliflower florets on one of the prepared sheet pans. Add the oil, smoked paprika, chipotle powder, cumin, and salt and toss until the cauliflower is evenly coated. Spread into a single layer and roast until the cauliflower is tender and golden brown, 20 to 25 minutes, tossing halfway through.

PREPARE THE TOSTADAS: On the other prepared sheet pan, place the tortillas in a single layer. Brush the tops of each of the tortillas with avocado oil, 1 teaspoon per tortilla. Bake until they are crisp and golden brown on the edges, about 9 minutes.

MEANWHILE, MAKE THE BLACK BEANS: In a medium saucepan, combine the black beans, broth, and salsa verde over medium heat. Cook, uncovered and stirring occasionally, until the beans are tender, about 10 minutes.

WHEN the beans are tender, remove them from the heat. Add the lime juice. Using the back of a fork or a potato masher, mash the beans coarsely. They do not need to be completely smooth, just mashed enough to spread on the tostadas.

TO SERVE: Spread some of the black bean mixture on each tostada. Add some the sliced avocado and a small handful of the arugula. Top with the roasted cauliflower and serve with lime wedges. Garnish as desired.

# tikka masala-inspired lentils

**MAKES 6 SERVINGS** • **TOTAL TIME: 45 MINUTES**

2 tablespoons extra-virgin olive oil

2 cups fine-diced yellow onion (about 1 large onion)

1 teaspoon kosher salt, plus more to taste

½ teaspoon freshly ground black pepper

2 garlic cloves, minced

One ½-inch piece fresh ginger, peeled and finely grated

1 tablespoon curry powder

1 teaspoon ground cumin

1 teaspoon paprika

1 teaspoon ground turmeric

½ teaspoon cayenne pepper

½ teaspoon ground cinnamon

One 6-ounce can tomato paste

2 cups brown lentils, rinsed

4 cups low-sodium vegetable broth

1 bay leaf

One 13-ounce can unsweetened full-fat coconut milk

2 tablespoons freshly squeezed lemon juice (about 1 lemon)

Prepared cauliflower rice or steamed rice, for serving

Fresh cilantro leaves, for serving

*Tikka masala is traditionally made with chicken, but this meatless version is the perfect, pantry-friendly dinner that is both healthy and hearty. Packed with flavor from the combination of fragrant spices, coconut milk, and tomato paste, this dinner comes together in under an hour and will be a new go-to on the busy nights when you need to rely on your pantry to do the work.*

IN a large pot or Dutch oven, heat the oil over medium heat. Add the onion, salt, black pepper, garlic, and ginger and sauté, stirring, until the onion is tender, about 4 minutes.

ADD the curry powder, cumin, paprika, turmeric, cayenne, cinnamon, and tomato paste. Toast the spices, stirring, until very fragrant, about 2 minutes. Add the lentils and stir to incorporate.

WHILE stirring, add the broth. Mix well, add the bay leaf, and bring to a boil. Reduce the heat to a simmer, cover, and cook, stirring occasionally, until the lentils are almost tender, about 20 minutes. They should still have a little bit of a bite to them at this point in the cooking process.

ADD the coconut milk and stir to combine. Cook, uncovered and stirring often, until the lentils are tender but not mushy, 5 to 10 more minutes. Stir in the lemon juice. Taste and adjust the salt as desired.

SERVE with the prepared rice and top with fresh cilantro.

# roasted vegetable pita with herby tahini

GLUTEN-FREE

DAIRY-FREE

VEGETARIAN

**MAKES 2 SERVINGS** • **TOTAL TIME: 45 MINUTES**

## FOR THE ROASTED VEGETABLES

2 red bell peppers, cut into ½-inch-wide strips

1 large zucchini, cut into ¼-inch-thick slices

1 small red onion, cut into ¼-inch-thick rounds

2 tablespoons extra-virgin olive oil

½ to 1 teaspoon kosher salt (see note on page 150)

½ teaspoon freshly ground black pepper

1 teaspoon za'atar seasoning

## FOR THE ROASTED CHICKPEAS

One 15-ounce can chickpeas, drained, rinsed, and patted dry

1½ tablespoons extra-virgin olive oil

½ teaspoon kosher salt

½ teaspoon garlic powder

½ teaspoon paprika

¼ teaspoon cayenne pepper, optional

½ teaspoon dried oregano

## FOR THE HERBY TAHINI

¼ cup tahini

¼ cup freshly squeezed lemon juice (about 2 lemons)

2 tablespoons extra-virgin olive oil

2 garlic cloves, roughly chopped

¼ cup fresh cilantro leaves

¼ cup roughly torn fresh dill fronds

¼ teaspoon kosher salt

¼ teaspoon freshly ground black pepper

*One of my favorite vegetarian meals is a simple veggie sandwich. Instead of making the traditional version, here I amp things up by roasting some veggies and chickpeas in Mediterranean spices, making a truly epic herby tahini sauce, and serving it all up in a warmed pita pocket. It's one of my favorite ways to have an extra filling meal with plenty of veggies and nutrients!*

PREHEAT the oven to 400°F. Line two large sheet pans with parchment paper.

PREPARE THE VEGETABLES: Combine the bell peppers, zucchini, and red onion in a single layer on one of the prepared sheet pans. Drizzle evenly with the oil and season with the salt, black pepper, and za'atar seasoning. Toss, then spread into a single layer and set aside.

PREPARE THE CHICKPEAS: On the other sheet pan, add the chickpeas. Drizzle with the oil and season with salt, garlic powder, paprika, cayenne (if using), and oregano. Toss, then spread into a single layer.

SET the pans with the vegetables and chickpeas on separate oven racks and roast until the vegetables are golden and the chickpeas are tender and slightly crisp, about 20 minutes. Remove the chickpeas. Set the oven to broil and broil the vegetables for 1 to 2 minutes until a golden brown crust forms, watching carefully so they do not burn.

MAKE THE HERBY TAHINI: In a blender or using an immersion blender in a wide-mouth jar, combine the herby tahini ingredients and process until smooth. If the dressing is too thick, add warm water 1 tablespoon at a time until the sauce is smooth and creamy. Set aside.

TO SERVE: Spread some tahini sauce inside each pita half. Add the sliced tomato, lettuce, alfalfa sprouts, cucumber, roasted chickpeas, and roasted vegetables. Top with dill fronds.

2 gluten-free pita breads, sliced in half

1 Roma (plum) tomato, halved and thinly sliced

2 cups thinly sliced romaine lettuce

4 ounces alfalfa sprouts

½ English cucumber, thinly sliced

Fresh dill fronds, for garnish

# spicy blistered green beans

**MAKES 4 SERVINGS** • **TOTAL TIME: 20 MINUTES**

1 tablespoon toasted sesame oil

2 tablespoons avocado oil, divided

1 pound green beans, ends trimmed

1 teaspoon kosher salt, plus more to taste

2 cups medium-diced baby bella mushrooms

2 garlic cloves, minced

1-inch piece fresh ginger, peeled and finely grated

1 teaspoon crushed red pepper flakes, plus more for serving (optional)

2 tablespoons coconut aminos

1 tablespoon rice vinegar

2 teaspoons coconut sugar

2 cups prepared cauliflower rice or steamed rice

*Beautifully blistered green beans are tossed in a spicy, savory, garlicky sauce and ready in a flash. This Chinese-inspired dish could certainly be a side dish, but this is also one of my go-to meatless meals. The mushrooms make it feel a little bit meatier, and I love the texture they add to the slightly crispy green beans.*

IN a large skillet, heat the sesame oil and 1 tablespoon of the avocado oil over medium-high heat. Add the green beans and salt and cook, tossing often, until the beans are blistered but remain slightly crunchy, about 8 minutes. Remove the beans from the skillet and set aside.

REDUCE the heat to medium and add the remaining 1 tablespoon avocado oil along with the mushrooms, garlic, ginger, and pepper flakes. Toss to combine. Cook the mushrooms without stirring to let them get a good sear, about 3 minutes. Add the coconut aminos, rice vinegar, and coconut sugar and cook, stirring often, until the mushrooms are tender and the sauce has reduced by half, about 2 minutes.

RETURN the green beans to the skillet and toss to combine. Cook and continue to stir, until the beans are heated through and well coated in the sauce, about 2 more minutes. Taste and add more salt, if needed.

SERVE over the prepared rice and garnish with more pepper flakes, if desired.

# spaghetti squash with sun-dried tomatoes and mushrooms

**MAKES 4 SERVINGS** • **TOTAL TIME: 50 MINUTES**

2 small spaghetti squashes
(1 to 2 pounds each)

3 tablespoons extra-virgin olive oil,
divided

1½ teaspoons kosher salt, divided

¼ cup pine nuts

3 cups thinly sliced stemmed shiitake
mushrooms

2 garlic cloves, minced

½ teaspoon freshly ground black
pepper

½ teaspoon crushed red pepper flakes

One 7-ounce jar oil-packed sun-dried
tomatoes, drained and thinly sliced
(about 1 cup)

2 cups baby spinach

½ cup torn fresh basil leaves

1 tablespoon freshly squeezed lemon
juice (about ½ lemon)

3 ounces crumbled goat cheese, plus
more for serving

*Spaghetti squash tossed with sun-dried tomatoes and shiitake mushrooms is a flavorful and naturally gluten-free and low-carb recipe to enjoy any night of the week. While the spaghetti squash takes about 30 minutes to roast, once it's ready, this dinner comes together in no time with simple ingredients that result in a beautiful and nutritious meal.*

PREHEAT the oven to 400°F. Line a sheet pan with parchment paper.

ROAST THE SPAGHETTI SQUASH: Trim the ends of the spaghetti squash and halve it crosswise. Using a sharp spoon or ice cream scoop, scoop out the seeds and stringy bits from the center of each cavity and discard. Brush the inside of the halves all over with 1 tablespoon of the oil and season with ½ teaspoon of the salt. Place the squash cut side down on the prepared sheet pan and roast until fork-tender, about 30 minutes. Set aside until cool enough to handle.

MEANWHILE, in a dry (no oil) large deep skillet, toast the pine nuts over medium heat, tossing often until toasted and fragrant, 2 to 3 minutes. Watch carefully so they don't burn. Remove from the skillet and set aside.

IN the same skillet used for the pine nuts, heat the remaining 2 tablespoons of oil over medium-high heat. Add the mushrooms in a single layer and let them sear on one side, undisturbed, for 2 to 3 minutes.

WHEN the mushrooms are golden, reduce the heat to medium. Add the garlic, the remaining 1 teaspoon of salt, black pepper, and pepper flakes, and sauté, stirring, until the garlic is golden, about 1 minute. Add the sun-dried tomatoes and sauté for 1 minute. Reduce the heat to low and keep warm while you shred the squash.

WHEN the squash is cool enough to handle, use a fork to gently scrape out the strands so that they resemble spaghetti. Add the squash strands to the skillet along with the spinach and toss until the spinach is wilted and the squash is well combined with the mushrooms and sun-dried tomatoes.

ADD the basil, lemon juice, and goat cheese and toss until the goat cheese is melted and evenly coats the spaghetti squash.

DIVIDE among four bowls and top with the toasted pine nuts and additional goat cheese.

# red pepper miso buddha bowls

**MAKES 4 SERVINGS** • **TOTAL TIME: 40 MINUTES**

### FOR THE SWEET POTATOES

1 large unpeeled sweet potato, cut into 1-inch cubes

2 tablespoons extra-virgin olive oil

1 teaspoon kosher salt

½ teaspoon freshly ground black pepper

### FOR THE RED PEPPER MISO DRIZZLE

½ cup roughly chopped jarred roasted red pepper (about 1 pepper)

¼ cup coconut aminos

2 tablespoons no-sugar-added sriracha (I use Yellowbird brand)

2 tablespoons rice vinegar

1½ tablespoons gluten-free white miso (see page 9)

1 garlic clove, peeled

### FOR THE CUCUMBERS

2 cups medium-diced Persian (mini) cucumbers (about 4 cucumbers)

2 tablespoons rice vinegar

1 tablespoon extra-virgin olive oil

1 teaspoon black sesame seeds

¼ teaspoon kosher salt

### FOR THE MUSHROOMS AND KALE

3 tablespoons extra-virgin olive oil, divided

4 cups sliced baby bella mushrooms

¾ teaspoon kosher salt, divided

8 cups deribbed and roughly chopped lacinato kale (about 2 bunches)

2 tablespoons freshly squeezed lemon juice (about 1 lemon)

### FOR SERVING

2 cups cooked grain (I use quinoa, brown rice, or farro)

1 large avocado, thinly sliced

*A Buddha bowl is generally a dish that consists of small portions of several different foods; typically, a grain, vegetable, protein, and dressing. This particular bowl, inspired by Flower Child restaurant's Mother Earth Bowl, is packed with all sorts of nutritious goodness, and amped with flavor from the red pepper miso drizzle. While there are a few pots, pans, and bowls involved in creating this recipe, it is simple to make and absolutely wonderful in every way.*

**ROAST THE SWEET POTATOES:** Preheat the oven to 375°F. Line a large sheet pan with parchment paper.

**PLACE** the sweet potatoes on the prepared sheet pan. Drizzle with the oil, sprinkle with the salt and black pepper, and toss to coat. Parbake for 15 minutes.

**MEANWHILE, MAKE THE RED PEPPER MISO DRIZZLE:** In a blender or using an immersion blender in a wide-mouth jar, combine the drizzle ingredients and blend until smooth. Set aside.

**WHEN** the sweet potato cook time is complete, remove the pan from the oven and drizzle the sweet potatoes with ½ cup of the red pepper miso drizzle. Toss until the sweet potatoes are well coated. Return the pan to the oven and roast until they are tender and golden on the edges, 10 to 15 minutes.

**PREPARE THE CUCUMBERS:** In a medium bowl, combine all the cucumber ingredients. Toss to combine and set aside.

**COOK THE MUSHROOMS AND KALE:** In a large skillet, heat 2 tablespoons of the oil over medium heat. Add the mushrooms and ½ teaspoon of the salt. Cook, undisturbed, until golden on one side, 2 to 3 minutes. Flip and continue to cook until the mushrooms are tender and golden on all the edges, 3 to 4 more minutes. Transfer to a bowl and set aside.

**IN** the same skillet, combine the remaining 1 tablespoon oil, the kale, and the remaining ¼ teaspoon salt. Cook, tossing, until the kale has just wilted, 2 to 3 minutes. Add the lemon juice, toss, and remove from the heat.

**TO SERVE:** Divide the cooked grain among four bowls. Top with the mushrooms, kale, and cucumbers. Add the sweet potatoes and drizzle with a bit more of the red pepper miso drizzle. Top with sliced avocado.

# sheet pan ratatouille with crispy gnocchi

DAIRY-FREE

VEGETARIAN

*if modified:*
GLUTEN-FREE

**MAKES 4 SERVINGS • TOTAL TIME: 40 MINUTES**

## FOR THE RATATOUILLE

1 medium eggplant, cut into ½-inch cubes (about 4 cups)

2 cups halved cherry tomatoes

1 cup medium-diced yellow onion (about ½ large onion)

1 cup medium-diced zucchini (about 1 medium zucchini)

1 red bell pepper, cut into ½-inch squares

6 garlic cloves, peeled and smashed

3 tablespoons extra-virgin olive oil

1 tablespoon balsamic vinegar

1½ teaspoons kosher salt

1 teaspoon freshly ground black pepper

¼ teaspoon crushed red pepper flakes

1 teaspoon dried oregano

## FOR THE GNOCCHI

16 ounces shelf-stable gnocchi (see note; sub gluten-free gnocchi for gluten-free)

3 tablespoons extra-virgin olive oil

½ teaspoon kosher salt

¼ teaspoon freshly ground black pepper

## TO FINISH

1 tablespoon balsamic vinegar

¼ cup thinly sliced fresh basil leaves, plus more for serving

Crushed red pepper flakes, optional

*Cooking ratatouille in the oven is not only easier, but I also love the caramelized flavor that roasting adds to the vegetables! In this recipe, I add a second sheet pan of store-bought gnocchi. Typically, the instructions tell you to boil them, but roasting is the real winner. Direct heat from the oven with a little bit of olive oil helps them get crisp on the outside while remaining chewy and tender on the inside.*

SET one oven rack in the center and another rack in the second highest position of the oven. Preheat the oven to 450°F. Line two sheet pans with parchment paper.

PREPARE THE RATATOUILLE: On one of the prepared sheet pans, combine the eggplant, tomatoes, onion, zucchini, bell pepper, and garlic. Drizzle with the oil and balsamic vinegar. Sprinkle with the salt, black pepper, pepper flakes, and oregano. Toss until the veggies are well coated, then spread into a single layer. Set aside.

PREPARE THE GNOCCHI: On the other prepared sheet pan, spread the gnocchi. Drizzle with the oil and season with the salt and black pepper. Spread into a single layer.

PLACE the gnocchi on the second-highest oven rack and the ratatouille on the one below it. Bake until the veggies are roasted and the gnocchi are browned and crisped, 20 to 25 minutes, tossing the contents of each sheet pan halfway through the cooking process. Remove the pans from the oven.

TO FINISH: Toss the ratatouille with the balsamic and fresh basil. Divide the ratatouille among four bowls and top with the gnocchi. Garnish with additional basil and pepper flakes (if using).

## FROM MY KITCHEN TO YOURS

This recipe uses the gnocchi you can find in the dried pasta section of your grocery store. Please note that cauliflower gnocchi will not work well, as their water content is too high for them to crisp. If you prefer cauliflower gnocchi, I suggest making the ratatouille as noted here and then topping with cauliflower gnocchi prepared according to the package directions.

# portobello tacos with serrano avocado crema

**MAKES 4 SERVINGS** • **TOTAL TIME: 35 MINUTES**

### FOR THE SERRANO AVOCADO CREMA

1 large avocado

1 serrano pepper, seeded and roughly chopped

¼ cup fresh cilantro leaves

3 tablespoons freshly squeezed lime juice (about 1½ limes)

3 tablespoons unsweetened full-fat coconut milk (sub Greek yogurt if you are not dairy-free)

1 tablespoon extra-virgin olive oil

½ teaspoon kosher salt

½ teaspoon freshly ground black pepper

### FOR THE SLAW

5 cups thinly shredded red cabbage (about 1 small head)

1 tablespoon extra-virgin olive oil

1 tablespoon freshly squeezed lime juice (about ½ lime)

¼ teaspoon kosher salt

### FOR THE MUSHROOMS

4 large portobello mushrooms, cleaned and cut into ½-inch-wide slices

3 tablespoons extra-virgin olive oil, divided, plus more as needed

1 tablespoon tapioca flour

1 tablespoon coconut aminos

½ teaspoon ground cumin

1 teaspoon chili powder

½ teaspoon dried oregano

½ teaspoon kosher salt

½ teaspoon freshly ground black pepper

### FOR SERVING

8 grain-free tortillas (I use Siete brand)

6 radishes, cut into matchsticks

Fresh cilantro leaves

*With their juicy, meaty texture, portobello mushrooms are my favorite plant-based taco filling. I season them here with some of my favorite go-to seasonings for tacos and add coconut aminos to help bring out their savory flavor. The serrano avocado crema spices up the "meaty" mushroom filling for a great taco night!*

**MAKE THE SERRANO AVOCADO CREMA:** In a blender or using an immersion blender in a wide-mouth jar, combine the crema ingredients and blend until smooth. Set aside.

**MAKE THE SLAW:** In a medium bowl, combine the slaw ingredients and toss to combine. Set aside.

**COOK THE MUSHROOMS:** In a medium bowl, combine the sliced mushrooms, 1 tablespoon of the oil, and the tapioca flour. Gently toss to coat. In a large skillet (preferably cast-iron), heat the remaining 2 tablespoons oil over medium-high heat until the oil just begins to shimmer. Working in batches so as not to overcrowd the pan, add the mushrooms in a single layer and cook until golden brown on both sides, 2 to 3 minutes per side. Add more oil to the pan for the additional batches if it becomes dry. Transfer the cooked mushrooms to a plate as you finish the batches.

**RETURN** all the mushrooms to the pan and reduce the heat to medium-low. Add the coconut aminos and season with the cumin, chili powder, oregano, salt, and black pepper. Toss gently to combine, allowing the sauce to caramelize, about 2 minutes. Remove from the heat and set aside.

**TO SERVE:** One at a time, place the tortillas in a dry (no oil) stainless steel skillet over medium heat and cook for about 30 seconds on each side. (Alternatively, you can char the tortillas directly over a gas flame for a few seconds using tongs.)

**FOR** each taco, place a small amount of the slaw on a warm tortilla and add 3 or 4 mushroom slices. Top with a dollop of the crema, then add some radish matchsticks and cilantro leaves.

217    EASY PALEO CHOCOLATE BANANA BREAD

218    STRAWBERRY OATMEAL BARS

221    CHOCOLATE CHUNK COOKIE SKILLET

222    ONE-POT GRAIN-FREE BROWNIES

225    CADY'S CARROT CAKE

228    NO-BAKE CHOCOLATE PEANUT BUTTER BARS

231    STRAWBERRY SHORT-CRISPIES

desserts

# easy paleo chocolate banana bread

GLUTEN-FREE

DAIRY-FREE

PALEO

GRAIN-FREE

VEGETARIAN

MAKES 1 LOAF  •  TOTAL TIME: 1 HOUR 35 MINUTES

Nonstick cooking spray

1 cup mashed very ripe banana
(3 to 4 medium bananas)

½ cup pure maple syrup

2 large eggs, at room temperature

⅓ cup liquid coconut oil (see note)

2 teaspoons pure vanilla extract

1 teaspoon instant espresso powder

1½ teaspoons ground cinnamon

½ cup unsweetened cocoa powder

1 cup tapioca flour

1¼ cups super-fine almond flour

1½ teaspoons baking soda

¼ teaspoon kosher salt

½ cup plus 1 tablespoon dairy-free
semisweet chocolate chips

½ teaspoon flaky sea salt, optional

*If you grew up on the jumbo chocolate muffins from Costco, this will taste very similar, but it won't be followed by a sugar crash. The almond flour and tapioca base create a perfectly light and flavorful loaf that you would never guess is gluten-free. And it's even better the next day toasted and paired with a cup of coffee!*

SET a rack in the center of the oven and preheat the oven to 350°F. Line a loaf pan with parchment paper, letting it hang over the two long sides of the pan (you'll use it to lift out the loaf later), and lightly mist it with cooking spray.

IN a large bowl, combine the banana, maple syrup, eggs, coconut oil, and vanilla. Whisk together until very well combined.

ADD the instant espresso powder, cinnamon, cocoa powder, tapioca flour, almond flour, baking soda, and kosher salt. Mix until well combined and lump-free. Gently fold in ½ cup of the chocolate chips.

POUR the batter into the prepared loaf pan and spread it into an even layer. Sprinkle the remaining 1 tablespoon chocolate chips over the top.

TRANSFER the loaf to the oven and bake until a knife can be inserted into the center of the loaf and it comes out mostly clean, 45 to 55 minutes.

SPRINKLE the loaf with the flaky salt (if using) and let cool in the pan for 20 minutes, then gently remove it and transfer it to a wire rack to cool completely. Slice with a serrated knife.

TO store, let cool completely and keep in an airtight container at room temperature for up to 5 days. It's also great to pop into the freezer and store for later!

## FROM MY KITCHEN TO YOURS

FOR COCONUT OIL: I prefer using liquid coconut oil, which I find in the baking aisle of my local grocery store, but if you cannot find it, you can melt solid coconut oil and let it cool before using or use avocado oil.

TO MAKE MUFFINS: Adjust to only ½ teaspoon of baking soda and add 2 teaspoons of baking powder. Line a muffin pan with liners and fill ¾ of the way full. Bake at 350°F for about 20 minutes.

# strawberry oatmeal bars

**MAKES 12 BARS** • **TOTAL TIME: 1 HOUR 10 MINUTES**

Nonstick cooking spray

1½ cups quick oats

1 cup super-fine almond flour

1 cup tapioca flour

¼ cup coconut sugar

½ teaspoon ground cinnamon

1 teaspoon baking powder

¼ teaspoon kosher salt

½ cup liquid coconut oil (see note, page 217)

⅔ cup pure maple syrup

2 tablespoons creamy unsweetened almond butter

1 teaspoon pure vanilla extract

One 10-ounce jar strawberry preserves or your preferred preserves

Nondairy vanilla ice cream, optional for serving

*This easy sweet treat is both delicious and versatile. It's the perfect dessert to pop into lunch boxes, to eat on the go for breakfast, or to serve warm for a dinner party with a scoop of ice cream. You can also get creative with the type of preserves that you choose for the middle layer! Strawberry or raspberry are the go-to in our household, but we also love to use peach preserves for a festive summer dessert.*

PREHEAT the oven to 350°F. Line a 9 × 9-inch baking pan with parchment paper, letting it hang over two opposite sides of the pan (you'll use it to lift out the bars later), and lightly mist it with cooking spray.

IN a large bowl, combine the oats, almond flour, tapioca flour, coconut sugar, cinnamon, baking powder, and salt. Stir to combine and break up any clumps. Set aside.

IN a separate medium bowl, combine the coconut oil, maple syrup, almond butter, and vanilla and whisk until smooth.

POUR the coconut oil mixture into the oat mixture and stir to combine. The texture should be somewhere between cookie dough and brownie batter.

SPOON about three-quarters of the oat mixture into the prepared pan and smooth it out into an even layer (reserving the rest for topping later). Bake until just set and lightly golden, 20 minutes.

REMOVE from the oven. Carefully dollop the strawberry preserves over the bottom oat layer and use a rubber spatula to spread it out in an even layer. Using your hands, evenly crumble the reserved oat mixture over the preserves (you don't need to cover the whole surface). Return to the oven and bake until the crumble on top is golden brown, about 25 minutes.

LET rest in the pan for 15 minutes. Carefully lift it out of the pan and allow to cool completely before cutting into 12 bars. Serve warm as is or with a scoop of nondairy vanilla ice cream, if desired.

TO store, let cool completely and keep in an airtight container at room temperature for up to 3 days.

# chocolate chunk cookie skillet

**MAKES 10 SERVINGS** • **TOTAL TIME: 1 HOUR 5 MINUTES**

GLUTEN-FREE

DAIRY-FREE

PALEO

GRAIN-FREE

VEGETARIAN

Nonstick cooking spray

1 tablespoon pure vanilla extract

2 large eggs, at room temperature

1 cup coconut sugar

½ cup pure maple syrup

½ cup liquid coconut oil (see note, page 217)

½ teaspoon ground cinnamon

3 cups super-fine almond flour

1½ cups tapioca flour

¼ teaspoon kosher salt

1 teaspoon baking soda

1¼ cups dairy-free chocolate chunks (I use Hu Gems)

½ teaspoon flaky sea salt, optional

Nondairy vanilla ice cream, optional for serving

*If you've ever enjoyed a Pizookie from BJ's Restaurant, you're going to love this homemade, paleo rendition. This recipe is basically a giant chocolate chip cookie baked in a skillet, which creates perfectly chewy edges and a warm, ooey-gooey center. You'll also save time by not having to scoop the dough into individual cookies, making it much easier to make and share with a crowd! Serve it with scoops of vanilla ice cream for the classic Pizookie experience.*

SET an oven rack in the center position and preheat the oven to 350°F. Line an 8-inch cast-iron skillet with a round of parchment paper fitted to the bottom of the pan and lightly mist it with cooking spray.

IN a large bowl, combine the vanilla, eggs, coconut sugar, maple syrup, and coconut oil. Whisk until very well combined, 1 to 2 minutes.

ADD the cinnamon, almond flour, tapioca flour, kosher salt, and baking soda to the bowl and stir until well combined. Fold in ¾ cup of the chocolate chunks.

POUR the batter into the prepared skillet. Top with the remaining ½ cup chocolate chunks, gently pressing them into the top of the batter.

BAKE for 20 minutes, uncovered, until the cookie begins to turn golden brown. After 20 minutes, carefully tent the skillet with a sheet of foil. This method ensures the center of the cookie cooks a bit more, but the cookie does not get too browned on top. Continue to bake until the cookie is golden and a bit crisp on the edges but still slightly gooey in the center, another 10 minutes. If you test the cookie with a cake tester, the tester will not come out clean. This is fine. The cookie will continue to cook as it rests outside the oven.

REMOVE from the oven and sprinkle with flaky salt (if using). Rest in the pan for 25 minutes before serving. This cookie skillet is best served fresh and warm (it will still be warm even after resting). If desired, top with scoops of nondairy vanilla ice cream.

# one-pot grain-free brownies

**MAKES 12 BROWNIES** • **TOTAL TIME: 55 MINUTES**

Nonstick cooking spray

1 stick (4 ounces) unsalted butter (sub vegan butter for dairy-free)

⅔ cup semisweet chocolate chips (sub dairy-free chocolate chips for dairy-free)

¼ cup unsweetened creamy cashew butter or almond butter

⅔ cup pure maple syrup

1 cup coconut sugar

1 teaspoon pure vanilla extract

4 large eggs, at room temperature

3 tablespoons unsweetened cocoa powder

2 teaspoons instant espresso powder

1 cup tapioca flour

¼ teaspoon kosher salt

½ cup chocolate chunks or large chocolate chips, optional (I use Hu Gems for a dairy-free option)

½ teaspoon flaky sea salt, optional

*Brownies are one of my all-time favorite desserts. These easy, homemade brownies taste similar to box brownies, in a good way, but even better— and I promise they are just as easy! You need only one saucepan, and you don't even need a mixer! Made with grain-free ingredients and no refined sugars, these brownies come out perfectly chewy and fudgy (but not too fudgy). They are destined to become a family favorite!*

SET a rack in the center of the oven and preheat the oven to 350°F. Line a 9 × 13-inch baking pan with parchment paper, letting it hang over the two long sides of the pan (you'll use it to lift out the brownies later). Lightly mist it with cooking spray.

IN a medium saucepan, combine the butter, chocolate chips, cashew butter, and maple syrup. Cook over medium-low heat, stirring constantly, until the mixture is melted and smooth, about 4 minutes, taking care not to burn it.

REMOVE from the heat. Stir in the coconut sugar and vanilla until well combined and smooth. Add the eggs and whisk until very smooth, for about 1 minute. (Whisking the eggs helps the brownies rise and get that signature crackly top!) Add the cocoa powder, espresso powder, tapioca flour, and kosher salt and whisk again until smooth.

POUR the batter into the prepared baking pan. Scatter the chocolate chunks (if using) over the top.

BAKE until the brownies have set or until a knife inserted in the center comes out with only a few crumbs attached, 25 to 30 minutes.

REMOVE from the oven and let rest in the pan for 10 minutes. Using the parchment paper sling, carefully lift and transfer the brownies to a wire rack and sprinkle with flaky salt (if using). Let cool for at least 10 more minutes before cutting into the brownies and serving.

TO store, let cool completely and keep in an airtight container at room temperature for up to 3 days.

# cady's carrot cake

**MAKES 9 SQUARES** • **TOTAL TIME: 1 HOUR 15 MINUTES**

## FOR THE CAKE

Nonstick cooking spray

2½ cups super-fine almond flour

1¼ cups tapioca flour

1 tablespoon ground cinnamon

1 teaspoon kosher salt

3 large eggs, at room temperature

¾ cup avocado oil

½ cup pure maple syrup

2½ teaspoons baking soda

1 teaspoon pure vanilla extract

1 teaspoon grated lemon zest

1 tablespoon freshly squeezed lemon juice (about ½ lemon)

½ teaspoon grated orange zest

2 cups shredded carrots (4 to 5 medium carrots; see note)

½ cup roughly chopped golden raisins

## FOR THE FROSTING

4 ounces cream cheese (sub nondairy cream cheese for dairy-free; I use Kite Hill brand), at room temperature

2 tablespoons unsalted butter (sub vegan butter for dairy-free), at room temperature

1½ teaspoons pure vanilla extract

1 tablespoon grated lemon zest

½ tablespoon freshly squeezed lemon juice (about ½ lemon)

2½ cups powdered sugar

## TO FINISH

¼ cup chopped toasted pecans

*I have dubbed this recipe "Cady's Carrot Cake" because it is truly one of her greatest masterpieces. If you don't know, Cady is the director of operations at The Defined Dish. Carrot cake is her husband's favorite dessert, and after making a family recipe over the years, she decided to try her hand at a grain-free and dairy-free rendition and absolutely nailed it. Cady, you're a real hero.*

MAKE THE CAKE: Preheat the oven to 350°F. Line a 9 × 9-inch baking pan with parchment paper, letting it hang over two opposite sides of the pan (you'll use it to lift out the cake later). Lightly mist it with cooking spray.

IN a medium bowl, sift together the almond flour, tapioca flour, cinnamon, and salt. Set aside.

IN a large bowl with a hand mixer or a stand mixer fitted with the whisk, beat the eggs on medium-high speed until pale yellow and fluffy, 3 to 4 minutes. Beat in the avocado oil, maple syrup, baking soda, vanilla, lemon zest, lemon juice, and orange zest. Beat on medium to combine.

ADJUST the mixer speed to medium-low and, working in 1-cup increments, slowly add the dry ingredients to the wet ingredients, scraping the sides of the bowl as needed. Mix until everything is well combined, 1 to 2 minutes.

SLOWLY add the shredded carrots and raisins to the batter and using a rubber spatula, fold in until well combined.

TIP the batter into the prepared baking pan, spreading the batter with a spatula if needed (see note). Bake until the top of the cake is lightly browned and a cake tester inserted into the middle comes out clean, about 35 minutes. If the top starts to get overly browned, place a sheet of foil over the top, but do note this is a darker cake.

LET the cake cool in the pan for 10 minutes, then use the parchment sling to carefully transfer the cake to a wire rack to cool completely.

*(recipe continues)*

**MEANWHILE, MAKE THE FROSTING:** In a stand mixer fitted with the paddle, combine the cream cheese, butter, vanilla, lemon zest, and lemon juice. Beat on medium speed until light and fluffy, 2 to 3 minutes. Slowly add the powdered sugar, beating on low at first to incorporate it. Continue to increase the speed and beat on high until well combined, 2 to 3 minutes. Transfer the frosting to the fridge until the cake is completely cooled.

**TO FINISH:** Top the cooled cake with the frosting, smoothing it out evenly with an offset spatula. Sprinkle the cake with the chopped pecans. Cut the cake into squares to serve. Store leftovers in an airtight container in the refrigerator for up to 3 days.

## FROM MY KITCHEN TO YOURS

**FOR CARROT SHREDDING:** After the carrots are washed and peeled, you can either hand-shred them or use a food processor with the shredding blade. Do not use preshredded carrots; they are too dry and do not have the moisture needed to help the cake come together.

**FOR THE BATTER:** This batter may be a bit thicker than a typical cake batter, but this is to account for the moisture the carrots will release in the oven.

# no-bake chocolate peanut butter bars

**MAKES 16 BARS** • **TOTAL TIME: 30 MINUTES** • **FREEZING TIME: 3 HOURS MINIMUM**

### FOR THE BASE

Nonstick cooking spray

1¼ cups raw, unsalted cashews

6 Medjool dates, pitted

½ teaspoon vanilla extract

¼ teaspoon kosher salt

### FOR THE PEANUT BUTTER LAYER

½ cup creamy peanut butter

¼ cup pure maple syrup

1 tablespoon liquid coconut oil

⅓ cup salted roasted peanuts, roughly chopped

### FOR THE CHOCOLATE LAYER

1 cup semisweet dairy-free chocolate chips

1 tablespoon liquid coconut oil

½ teaspoon flaky sea salt, optional for topping

**FROM MY KITCHEN TO YOURS**

I suggest cutting the bars while they're still frozen; they're much more delicate when they're at room temperature. To do so, you will need a very sharp knife. Run the knife under hot water first to make it easier to cut the bars.

*There's nothing like a no-bake sweet treat, especially in hot weather! These bars are a family favorite—the perfect bite to keep in the freezer for whenever your sweet tooth strikes.*

LINE an 8 × 8-inch baking pan with parchment paper, letting it hang over two opposite sides of the pan (you'll use it to lift out the bars later). Lightly mist it with cooking spray. Set aside.

MAKE THE BASE: Place the cashews in a small bowl and cover them with boiling water. Set aside for 10 minutes to soften. Drain the cashews and discard the water.

IN a food processor or high-powered blender, combine the soaked cashews, dates, vanilla, and salt. Pulse until you get a crumbly but pasty mixture. Scoop the base mixture into the prepared baking pan and press it into the bottom of the pan in an even, packed layer. It's helpful to use the bottom of a measuring cup that's been coated with cooking spray to get a super-flat base. Place in freezer for 10 minutes to let the layer set slightly.

MAKE THE PEANUT BUTTER LAYER: In a medium bowl, combine the peanut butter, maple syrup, and coconut oil and stir until smooth. Pour the mixture on top of the base layer and spread it into an even layer. Sprinkle it evenly with the chopped peanuts, using your palm or the bottom of a measuring cup to gently press them into the peanut butter layer. Freeze for at least 15 minutes to let the layer set slightly.

MAKE THE CHOCOLATE LAYER: About 5 minutes before removing the pan from the freezer, melt the chocolate. In a microwave-safe bowl, combine the chocolate chips and coconut oil. Microwave in 30-second increments, stirring after each, until the mixture is completely melted and smooth, taking care not to burn it. Set aside to cool slightly.

REMOVE the base from the freezer. Carefully pour the melted chocolate over the peanuts and gently tilt the pan to distribute the chocolate evenly over the top, forming the top layer. Sprinkle with the flaky salt (if using).

FREEZE for at least 3 hours, preferably overnight. Cut into 16 bars (see note). Store in an airtight container in the freezer for up to 3 months.

# strawberry short-crispies

**MAKES 18 TO 24 SQUARES** • **TOTAL TIME: ABOUT 1 HOUR 15 MINUTES**

2½ cups freeze-dried strawberries, divided

5½ cups brown rice crisp cereal (I use One Degree Organic Foods sprouted brown rice crisps; you can sub Rice Krispies if not gluten-free)

1 cup honey

1 cup unsalted creamy cashew butter

1 teaspoon pure vanilla extract

3 tablespoons liquid coconut oil, divided

¼ teaspoon kosher salt

Nonstick cooking spray, optional

1½ cups white chocolate chips

*If you love strawberry shortcake but don't want to spend the time to make a homemade cake, you're going to absolutely love this rice crispy treat rendition. Infused with strawberry flavor using store-bought freeze-dried strawberries and topped with a layer of white chocolate, these are simply irresistible!*

LINE a 9 × 13-inch baking pan with parchment paper, letting it hang over the long sides of the pan (you'll use it to lift out the bars later). Set aside.

PLACE 2 cups of the dried strawberries in a plastic bag, reserving the other ½ cup for garnishing. Using a meat mallet or the bottom of a heavy skillet, crush the strawberries into a fine powder, leaving a few larger pieces. In a large bowl, combine the crushed strawberries and rice crisp cereal. Set aside.

IN a medium saucepan, heat the honey over medium heat and bring it to a boil for just 1 minute, without stirring.

REMOVE the honey from the heat and add the cashew butter, vanilla, 2 tablespoons of the coconut oil, and the salt. Stir until smooth. Pour the honey mixture over the cereal mixture and stir until well combined.

TRANSFER the mixture to the prepared baking pan and press it into an even layer. It's helpful to use the bottom of a measuring cup that's been coated with cooking spray to get an even base. Set aside in the fridge to cool completely.

MEANWHILE, in a microwave-safe bowl, combine the white chocolate chips and the remaining 1 tablespoon coconut oil. Microwave in 30-second increments, stirring after each, until the mixture is completely melted and smooth, taking care not to overcook it, as the chocolate will separate.

POUR the white chocolate mixture over the rice crisp layer, carefully tilting the pan until the white chocolate is in an even layer. Using your hands, gently crush the remaining ½ cup freeze-dried strawberries and distribute evenly over the white chocolate.

TRANSFER to the fridge or freezer to cool completely before slicing, about 30 minutes in the freezer or 1 hour in the fridge.

USING the parchment sling, lift and transfer the bars to a cutting board. Cut it into 18 to 24 squares.

### FROM MY KITCHEN TO YOURS

Store in an airtight container on the counter for up to 7 days or in the freezer for up to 3 months.

# acknowledgments

To the Defined Dish community, especially those who have been with me from the beginning, I am so happy that you continue to love, support, and trust me in your kitchens. You are the real reason I continue to write these books, and seeing you set the table to enjoy these dishes with the ones you love lights my soul on fire. From the bottom of my heart, thank you!

Clayton, I am constantly grateful for your taste-testing skills, your over-the-top ideas (which usually don't make it into my books), and your constant love for me. You always have a way of lifting me up when I am down, and I love you for that and so much more.

Sutton and Winnie, everything I do is with you in my heart. I hope by watching me pursue my dreams you are inspired to do the same in your lives. You are the loves of my life, and I am truly the luckiest mommy in the world.

To my right hand, Cady Grable, first and foremost, this book and The Defined Dish wouldn't be what they are today without you by my side. You are my wing woman, my work wife, my travel buddy, and truly so much more. Thank you for keeping me sane, for being an amazing taste tester, and for coming to the table with wonderful ideas. But most important, thank you for being my friend.

To my literary agent, Nicole Tourtelot, thank you for always going to bat for me and for answering every call, text, and email I send your way. You are a force at what you do and I am so grateful to work with you.

To the talented McKenzie Mitchell, who rolled up her sleeves and helped me test all one hundred of these delicious recipes. Your attention to detail and incredible notes are part of every recipe in this book. Thank you for working with me and for being so outstanding.

To Adam Pearson, what a joy it is to be able to work with you. It is safe to say this book wouldn't be what it is without you. Thank you for your creative eye, your talented hands, and, most important, for being ridiculously wonderful to work with. Thank you for bringing my recipes to life!

To my incredibly talented friend Kristen Kilpatrick, what a joy it has been to create my cookbooks with you behind the camera. Thank you for capturing me, my family, and my food in a way that feels completely true to me.

To Abby Pendergrast, thank you for your bold and beautiful taste, for perfectly curating the props for this book, and for always being a delight on set!

To the rest of the photoshoot team, Mikey Santillan, Diana Kim, and Sophie Clark, thank you for all your hard work to make this book come to life.

To Daniel Blaylock-Napolitan, thank you for being my ever-talented glam squad. You are a true angel on Earth, and I am so grateful to have had you on set with me to help me look and feel my very best.

To Denise Hernandez, my amazing talent manager, your belief in me from day one is never forgotten. Thank you for being a huge part of all things Defined Dish, for your constant support, your incredible advice, your creative ideas, and your loyalty.

To my editor, Cassie Jones, thank you for believing in me over and over again. I am thrilled to have worked with you for the second time. Thank you for allowing me to create books that are true to me. I am forever thankful for your insight and guidance.

And to the entire William Morrow dream team (you know who you are), you always make me feel at ease, and I know that I am in the greatest hands. Thank you for putting so much time, effort, and creativity into this book.

To all my dedicated recipe testers, thank you for helping me get these recipes into the final state we see printed in these pages. Your feedback is invaluable, and I am so grateful for the time you took to test each recipe.

Mom and Dad, thank you for all of the incredible memories around our dinner table when I was growing up. They have shaped me into who I am today and inspire each recipe I create.

To all my incredible family and friends who ate each recipe I cooked and gave encouraging feedback throughout this process, thank you. I wouldn't be where I am today without your advice, love, and support.

## oven temperature equivalents

250°F = 120°C

275°F = 135°C

300°F = 150°C

325°F = 160°C

350°F = 180°C

375°F = 190°C

400°F = 200°C

425°F = 220°C

450°F = 230°C

475°F = 240°C

500°F = 260°C

## measurement equivalents

Measurements should always be level unless directed otherwise.

⅛ teaspoon = 0.5 mL

¼ teaspoon = 1 mL

½ teaspoon = 2 mL

1 teaspoon = 5 mL

1 tablespoon = 3 teaspoons = ½ fluid ounce = 15 mL

2 tablespoons = ⅛ cup = 1 fluid ounce = 30 mL

4 tablespoons = ¼ cup = 2 fluid ounces = 60 mL

5⅓ tablespoons = ⅓ cup = 3 fluid ounces = 80 mL

8 tablespoons = ½ cup = 4 fluid ounces = 120 mL

10⅔ tablespoons = ⅔ cup = 5 fluid ounces = 160 mL

12 tablespoons = ¾ cup = 6 fluid ounces = 180 mL

16 tablespoons = 1 cup = 8 fluid ounces = 240 mL

**universal conversion chart**

# index

NOTE: Page references in *italics* indicate photographs.

## A

Almond butter
  Skillet Chicken and Veggies with "Peanut" Sauce, 122–23, *123*

Almonds
  California Turkey Salad with Raspberry Vinaigrette, *16,* 17
  Shredded Kale Salad with Grapefruit and Seared Salmon, 14, *15*

Apples
  Curried Chicken and Kale Salad with Creamy Harissa Dressing, *20,* 21
  Deconstructed Waldorf Salad, *42,* 43
  Shredded Kale Salad with Grapefruit and Seared Salmon, 14, *15*

Artichokes
  Greek-Inspired Chicken and Orzo Bake, *128,* 129
  and Spinach, Creamy Goat Cheese Pasta with, *82,* 83

Arugula
  BLT Panzanella, *30,* 31
  California Turkey Salad with Raspberry Vinaigrette, *16,* 17
  Creamy Italian Chopped Salad, *34,* 35
  Deconstructed Waldorf Salad, *42,* 43
  Mediterranean Salmon Burgers with Cucumber-Feta Salad, 182, *183*
  Warm Farro Steak Salad, 32, *33*
  and White Bean Salad, Seared Tuna with, 18, *19*

Asparagus
  Greek-Inspired Chicken and Orzo Bake, *128,* 129

Avocado(s)
  Baked Salmon Sushi Bowls with Spicy Mayo, *172,* 173
  Cajun Cobb Salad with Shrimp, 36, *37*
  California Turkey Salad with Raspberry Vinaigrette, *16,* 17
  Chipotle Cauliflower Tostadas, 198, *199*
  Grilled Chicken Salad with Chili-Lime Dressing, 22, *23*
  Jerk-Inspired Chicken Tacos, *124,* 125
  Macho Salad, *38,* 39
  Serrano Crema, Portobello Tacos with, 212, *213*
  Slow Cooker or Pressure Cooker Beer-Braised Chicken Tacos, 116–17, *117*
  Slow Cooker or Pressure Cooker Gochujang Shredded Beef Bowls, *138,* 139–40
  Sweet Potato Fry Salad with Lemon-Tahini Dressing, 40, *41*

## B

Bacon
  BLT Panzanella, *30, 31*
  Cajun Cobb Salad with Shrimp, 36, *37*
  Grilled Chicken Salad with Chili-Lime Dressing, 22, *23*
  Loaded Potato Leek Soup, 62, *63*
Banana Chocolate Bread, Easy Paleo, *216,* 217
Bang Bang Shrimp Lettuce Wraps, *192,* 193
Barbecue sauce
  about, 5

Barbecue sauce *(continued)*
    Sheet Pan Mini BBQ-Cheddar Meatloaves with
        Sweet Potatoes and Brussels Sprouts, *158, 159*
    Skillet BBQ Chicken Quinoa Bake, *110,* 111
Bars
    Chocolate Peanut Butter, No-Bake, 228, *229*
    Strawberry Oatmeal, 218, *219*
    Strawberry Short-Crispies, *230,* 231
Basil
    Calabrian Chile Pasta Pomodoro, 92, *93*
    Lemon Pesto, 8
    -Tomato Tortellini and Sausage Soup, 66, *67*
Bean(s). *See also* Green Beans
    Black, Soup, Simple, 50, *51*
    Chipotle Cauliflower Tostadas, 198, *199*
    Curried Chili, *52,* 53
    Roasted Vegetable Pita with Herby Tahini, 202–3,
        *203*
    Skillet BBQ Chicken Quinoa Bake, *110,* 111
    White, and Arugula Salad, Seared Tuna with, 18,
        *19*
    White, and Fish Puttanesca, Roasted, 170, *171*
Beef
    and Broccoli Lo Mein, *90,* 91
    Curried Chili, *52,* 53
    Easy Italian Wedding Soup, *48,* 49
    Enchilada–Stuffed Acorn Squash, 164, *165*
    Gochujang Shredded, Bowls, Slow Cooker or
        Pressure Cooker, *138,* 139–40
    Herby Mediterranean Baked Meatballs, *146,* 147
    Italian Skirt Steak with Bursting Tomatoes, 136,
        *137*
    One-Skillet Lasagna, 80, *81*
    Philly Cheesesteak–Stuffed Mushrooms, *152,* 153
    Schwarma, Simple Skillet, 144, *145*
    Sheet Pan Mini BBQ-Cheddar Meatloaves with
        Sweet Potatoes and Brussels Sprouts, *158,* 159
    Stew, Spiced, Slow Cooker or Pressure Cooker,
        68–69, *69*
    Tacos, Crunchy Baked, 156–57, *157*
    Thai-Inspired Steak Salad, *26*27
    Warm Farro Steak Salad, *32,* 33
Beer-Braised Chicken Tacos, Slow Cooker or Pressure
    Cooker, 116–17, *117*
Bok choy
    Green Curry Chicken Soup, *64,* 65
    One-Pot Green Curry Veggie Noodles, 84, *85*

Bread, Easy Paleo Chocolate Banana, *216,* 217
Bread-based salads
    BLT Panzanella, *30,* 31
    Fattoush Salad with Creamy Feta Dressing, 28, *29*
    Macho Salad, *38,* 39
Broccoli
    and Beef Lo Mein, *90,* 91
    Skillet Chicken and Veggies with "Peanut" Sauce,
        122–23, *123*
Broccolini
    Sheet Pan Coconut-Crusted Fish with Honey-
        Chili Drizzle, 186, *187*
Brownies, One-Pot Grain-Free, 222, *223*
Brussels Sprouts
    Sheet Pan Hot Honey Dijon Chicken, *114,* 115
    and Sweet Potatoes, Sheet Pan Mini BBQ-
        Cheddar Meatloaves with, *158,* 159
Buddha Bowls, Red Pepper Miso, 208, *209*
Buffalo sauce
    about, 5
    Crispy Buffalo Chicken Lettuce Wraps with Blue
        Cheese Sauce, 102–3, *103*
Burgers, Mediterranean Salmon, with Cucumber-Feta
    Salad, 182, *183*

### C

Cabbage
    Crunchy Blackened Salmon Tacos with Serrano
        Slaw, 176–77, *177*
    and Pork Stir-Fry, Chili Oil, 154, *155*
    Portobello Tacos with Serrano Avocado Crema,
        212, *213*
    Thai-Inspired Steak Salad, *26*27
Cajun Cobb Salad with Shrimp, 36, *37*
Cajun Sausage and Rice Skillet, *134, 135*
Cake, Cady's Carrot, *224,* 225–26
California Turkey Salad with Raspberry Vinaigrette,
    *16,* 17
Carrot(s)
    Cake, Cady's, *224,* 225–26
    Chicken Pot Pie Chowder, 54, *55*
    Lemongrass Pork Lettuce Cups, 148–49, *149*
    Roasted, and Herb Drizzle, Za'atar-Crusted Lamb
        Chops with, 150, *151*
    Sichuan-Inspired Beef Stir-Fry, *166,* 167
    Slow Cooker or Pressure Cooker Spiced Beef
        Stew, 68–69, *69*

Cashew(s)
 Chicken Stir-Fry, 118, *119*
 Lemon Basil Pesto, 8
Cauliflower
 Sheet Pan Sausage and Sweet Piquanté Peppers, *142*, 143
 Tostadas, Chipotle, 198, *199*
Cheese
 Beef Enchilada–Stuffed Acorn Squash, 164, *165*
 Blue, Sauce, Crispy Buffalo Chicken Lettuce Wraps with, 102–3, *103*
 California Turkey Salad with Raspberry Vinaigrette, *16*, 17
 Chipotle Turkey–Stuffed Poblano Peppers, 112, *113*
 Creamy Goat, Pasta with Spinach and Artichokes, *82*, 83
 Creamy Italian Chopped Salad, *34*, 35
 Crunchy Baked Beef Tacos, 156–57, *157*
 Deconstructed Waldorf Salad, *42*, 43
 Fattoush Salad with Creamy Feta Dressing, 28, *29*
 Grilled Chicken Salad with Chili-Lime Dressing, *22*, *23*
 Jalapeño Tuna Cake Melts, *188*, 189
 Mediterranean Salmon Burgers with Cucumber-Feta Salad, 182, *183*
 One-Skillet Lasagna, 80, *81*
 Philly Cheesesteak–Stuffed Mushrooms, *152*, 153
 Roasted Shrimp, Cherry Tomato, and Feta Pasta, *74*, 75
 Sheet Pan Mini BBQ-Cheddar Meatloaves with Sweet Potatoes and Brussels Sprouts, *158*, 159
 Skillet BBQ Chicken Quinoa Bake, *110*, 111
 Sour Cream Chicken Enchiladas, *106*, 107
 Warm Farro Steak, *32*, *33*
Chicken
 Beer-Braised, Tacos, Slow Cooker or Pressure Cooker, 116–17, *117*
 Cacciatore, Skillet, *100*, 101
 Creamy Enchilada, Slow Cooker or Pressure Cooker, *120*, 121
 Crispy Buffalo, Lettuce Wraps with Blue Cheese Sauce, 102–3, *103*
 Curried, and Kale Salad with Creamy Harissa Dressing, *20*, 21
 Curry, Skillet with Sweet Potatoes, 104, *105*
 Deconstructed Waldorf Salad, *42*, 43

Enchiladas, Sour Cream, *106*, 107
 and Green Chile Rice Soup, *56*, 57
 Green Curry Soup, *64*, 65
 Grilled, Salad with Chili-Lime Dressing, 22, *23*
 Hot Honey Dijon, Sheet Pan, *114*, 115
 Macho Salad, *38*, *39*
 and Orzo Bake, Greek-Inspired, *128*, 129
 Piccata Meatballs, 126, *127*
 Pot Pie Chowder, 54, *55*
 Quinoa Bake, Skillet BBQ, *110*, 111
 and Rice, One-Pan Coconut-Lime, 98, *99*
 Stir-Fry, Cashew, 118, *119*
 Stir-Fry, Saucy Gochujang, 108, *109*
 Tacos, Jerk-Inspired, *124*, 125
 Tortilla Soup, The Best, 46, *47*
 2 a.m. Kimchi Noodles, 76, 77
 and Veggies, Skillet, with "Peanut" Sauce, 122–23, *123*
Chickpeas
 Curried Chili, *52*, *53*
 Roasted Vegetable Pita with Herby Tahini, 202–3, *203*
Chile(s)
 The Best Chicken Tortilla Soup, 46, *47*
 Calabrian, Pasta Pomodoro, 92, *93*
 Chipotle Turkey–Stuffed Poblano Peppers, 112, *113*
 Crunchy Baked Beef Tacos, 156–57, *157*
 Crunchy Blackened Salmon Tacos with Serrano Slaw, 176–77, *177*
 Green, Chicken and Rice Soup, *56*, 57
 Jalapeño Tuna Cake Melts, *188*, 189
 mild diced green, 9
 One-Pan Coconut-Lime Chicken and Rice, 98, *99*
 pickled jalapeños, 9
 Portobello Tacos with Serrano Avocado Crema, 212, *213*
 Slow Cooker or Pressure Cooker Beer-Braised Chicken Tacos, 116–17, *117*
 Sour Cream Chicken Enchiladas, *106*, 107
Chili, Curried, *52*, *53*
Chili Oil Pork and Cabbage Stir-Fry, 154, *155*
Chocolate
 Banana Bread, Easy Paleo, *216*, 217
 Chunk Cookie Skillet, *220*, 221
 One-Pot Grain-Free Brownies, 222, *223*
 Peanut Butter Bars, No-Bake, 228, *229*

Chowder, Chicken Pot Pie, 54, *55*

Cilantro
> Skillet Mojo Pork Tenderloin, 160, *161*
> Thai-Inspired Steak Salad, 26*27*
> Za'atar-Crusted Lamb Chops with Roasted Carrots and Herb Drizzle, 150, *151*

Coconut
> -Crusted Fish, Sheet Pan, with Honey-Chili Drizzle, 186, *187*
> -Lime Chicken and Rice, One-Pan, 98, *99*

Condiments, store-bought, 5–11

Cookie Skillet, Chocolate Chunk, 220, 221

Corn
> Macho Salad, *38, 39*
> Skillet BBQ Chicken Quinoa Bake, *110,* 111

Cucumber(s)
> Baked Salmon Sushi Bowls with Spicy Mayo, *172,* 173
> Fattoush Salad with Creamy Feta Dressing, 28, *29*
> -Feta Salad, Mediterranean Salmon Burgers with, 182, *183*
> Red Pepper Miso Buddha Bowls, 208, *209*
> Thai-Inspired Steak Salad, 26*27*

Curried Chicken and Kale Salad with Creamy Harissa Dressing, 20, 21

Curried Chili, *52, 53*

Curry, Easy Ground Lamb, *162, 163*

Curry Chicken Skillet with Sweet Potatoes, 104, *105*

Curry paste
> Green Curry Chicken Soup, *64, 65*
> One-Pot Green Curry Veggie Noodles, 84, *85*
> Skillet Chicken and Veggies with "Peanut" Sauce, 122–23, *123*
> Thai, about, 11

D

Dill
> Fattoush Salad with Creamy Feta Dressing, 28, *29*
> Za'atar-Crusted Lamb Chops with Roasted Carrots and Herb Drizzle, 150, *151*

E

Eggplant
> Sheet Pan Ratatouille with Crispy Gnocchi, *210,* 211

Eggs
> Cajun Cobb Salad with Shrimp, 36, *37*

Sheet Pan Salmon Niçoise, 24–25, *25*

Enchilada Chicken, Creamy, Slow Cooker or Pressure Cooker, *120,* 121

Enchiladas, Sour Cream Chicken, *106,* 107

Escarole
> Easy Italian Wedding Soup, *48,* 49

F

Farro
> Red Pepper Miso Buddha Bowls, 208, *209*
> Steak Salad, Warm, *32, 33*

Fattoush Salad with Creamy Feta Dressing, 28, *29*

Fish. *See also* Salmon
> Coconut-Crusted, Sheet Pan, with Honey-Chili Drizzle, 186, *187*
> Creamy Cajun, 174–75, *175*
> Harissa, en Papillote, 178, *179*
> Jalapeño Tuna Cake Melts, *188,* 189
> Red Snapper Veracruzana, 194, *195*
> Seared Tuna with White Bean and Arugula Salad, 18, *19*
> and White Bean Puttanesca, Roasted, 170, *171*

Fruits. *See specific fruits*

G

Ginger and Peanut Butter Ground Turkey Stir-Fry, 130, *131*

Gnocchi, Crispy, Sheet Pan Ratatouille with, *210,* 211

Gochujang
> about, 6
> Chicken Stir-Fry, Saucy, 108, *109*
> Shredded Beef Bowls, Slow Cooker or Pressure Cooker, *138,* 139–40
> 2 a.m. Kimchi Noodles, 76, 77

Grains. *See* Farro; Quinoa; Rice

Grapefruit and Seared Salmon, Shredded Kale Salad with, 14, *15*

Grapes
> Deconstructed Waldorf Salad, *42, 43*

Greek-Inspired Chicken and Orzo Bake, *128,* 129

Green Beans
> Harissa Fish en Papillote, 178, *179*
> Saucy Gochujang Chicken Stir-Fry, 108, *109*
> Sheet Pan Salmon Niçoise, 24–25, *25*
> Spicy Blistered, 204, *205*

Greens. *See also* Arugula; Kale; Lettuce; Spinach
> Easy Italian Wedding Soup, *48,* 49

## H

Harissa
  about, 6
  Dressing, Creamy, Curried Chicken and Kale Salad with, *20,* 21
  Fish en Papillote, 178, *179*
  Herby Mediterranean Baked Meatballs, *146,* 147
  Lamb Pasta, Herby, *78,* 79
Herb(s). *See also specific herbs*
  Drizzle and Roasted Carrots, Za'atar-Crusted Lamb Chops with, 150, *151*
Honey
  -Chili Drizzle, Sheet Pan Coconut-Crusted Fish with, 186, *187*
  Hot, Dijon Chicken, Sheet Pan, *114,* 115

## I

Italian Lentil Soup, *60,* 61
Italian Skirt Steak with Bursting Tomatoes, 136, *137*

## J

Jalapeños, pickled, about, 9
Jerk-Inspired Chicken Tacos, *124,* 125

## K

Kale
  Creamy Dijon Penne with Kielbasa, 88, *89*
  and Curried Chicken Salad with Creamy Harissa Dressing, *20,* 21
  Easy Italian Wedding Soup, *48,* 49
  Italian Lentil Soup, *60,* 61
  Red Pepper Miso Buddha Bowls, 208, *209*
  Shredded, Salad with Grapefruit and Seared Salmon, 14, *15*
  Sweet Potato Fry Salad with Lemon-Tahini Dressing, 40, *41*
  Tomato-Basil Tortellini and Sausage Soup, 66, *67*
Kimchi
  Noodles, 2 a.m., 76, 77
  Slow Cooker or Pressure Cooker Gochujang Shredded Beef Bowls, *138,* 139–40

## L

Lamb
  Chops, Za'atar-Crusted, with Roasted Carrots and Herb Drizzle, 150, *151*
  Ground, Curry, Easy, *162,* 163

Herby Mediterranean Baked Meatballs, *146,* 147
  Pasta, Herby Harissa, *78,* 79
Lasagna, One-Skillet, 80, *81*
Leek Potato Soup, Loaded, 62, *63*
Lemon
  Basil Pesto, 8
  -Tahini Dressing, Sweet Potato Fry Salad with, 40, *41*
Lemongrass Pork Lettuce Cups, 148–49, *149*
Lentil(s)
  Soup, Italian, *60,* 61
  Tikka Masala-Inspired, *200,* 201
Lettuce
  Cajun Cobb Salad with Shrimp, *36, 37*
  Creamy Italian Chopped Salad, *34, 35*
  Crispy Buffalo Chicken, Wraps with Blue Cheese Sauce, 102–3, *103*
  Cups, Lemongrass Pork, 148–49, *149*
  Fattoush Salad with Creamy Feta Dressing, 28, *29*
  Grilled Chicken Salad with Chili-Lime Dressing, 22, *23*
  Macho Salad, *38, 39*
  Sheet Pan Salmon Niçoise, 24–25, *25*
  Thai-Inspired Steak Salad, *26 27*
  Wraps, Bang Bang Shrimp, *192,* 193
Lime-Coconut Chicken and Rice, One-Pan, 98, *99*

## M

Macho Salad, *38, 39*
Mayo
  Homemade, 7
  Spicy, Baked Salmon Sushi Bowls with, *172,* 173
Meat. *See* Beef; Lamb; Pork
Meatballs
  Chicken Piccata, 126, *127*
  Herby Mediterranean Baked, *146,* 147
Meatloaves, Sheet Pan Mini BBQ-Cheddar, with Sweet Potatoes and Brussels Sprouts, *158,* 159
Mediterranean Salmon Burgers with Cucumber-Feta Salad, 182, *183*
Mint
  Fattoush Salad with Creamy Feta Dressing, 28, *29*
  Sun-Dried Tomato, and Pesto Pasta, *86,* 87
  Thai-Inspired Steak Salad, *26 27*
Miso
  about, 9
  Red Pepper Buddha Bowls, 208, *209*

Mojo Pork Tenderloin, Skillet, 160, *161*
Mushroom(s)
    Chicken Pot Pie Chowder, 54, *55*
    Green Curry Chicken Soup, *64,* 65
    One-Pot Green Curry Veggie Noodles, 84, *85*
    Philly Cheesesteak–Stuffed, *152, 153*
    Portobello Tacos with Serrano Avocado Crema,
        212, *213*
    Red Pepper Miso Buddha Bowls, 208, *209*
    Skillet Chicken Cacciatore, *100,* 101
    Spicy Blistered Green Beans, 204, *205*
    and Sun-Dried Tomatoes, Spaghetti Squash with,
        *206,* 207
    Tarragon Orzo-tto, *94,* 95
    Tom Yum–Inspired Shrimp Stir-Fry, *180,* 181
Mustard
    Creamy Dijon Penne with Kielbasa, 88, *89*
    Dijon, about, 6
    Sheet Pan Hot Honey Dijon Chicken, *114,* 115

**N**

Noodle(s)
    Beef and Broccoli Lo Mein, *90,* 91
    Green Curry Chicken Soup, *64,* 65
    Kimchi, 2 a.m., 76, 77
    One-Pot Green Curry Veggie, 84, *85*
    and Shrimp Soup, Aromatic, 58, *59*
Nuts. *See* Almonds; Cashew(s); Peanuts; Walnuts

**O**

Oatmeal Strawberry Bars, 218, *219*
Olives
    Creamy Italian Chopped Salad, *34,* 35
    Greek-Inspired Chicken and Orzo Bake, *128,* 129
    Red Snapper Veracruzana, 194, *195*
    Roasted Fish and White Bean Puttanesca, 170,
        *171*
    Saffron-Spiced Shrimp Skillet, *184,* 185
    Sheet Pan Salmon Niçoise, 24–25, *25*

**P**

Panzanella, BLT, *30,* 31
Pasta
    Creamy Dijon Penne with Kielbasa, 88, *89*
    Creamy Goat Cheese, with Spinach and
        Artichokes, *82,* 83
    Easy Italian Wedding Soup, *48,* 49

Herby Harissa Lamb, *78,* 79
One-Pot Butternut Squash and Sausage, 72, *73*
One-Skillet Lasagna, 80, *81*
Pomodoro, Calabrian Chile, 92, *93*
Roasted Shrimp, Cherry Tomato, and Feta, *74,* 75
Sun-Dried Tomato, Pesto, and Mint, *86,* 87
Tarragon Mushroom Orzo-tto, *94,* 95
Tomato-Basil Tortellini and Sausage Soup, 66, *67*
Peanut Butter
    Chocolate Bars, No-Bake, 228, *229*
    and Ginger Ground Turkey Stir-Fry, 130, *131*
Peanuts
    No-Bake Chocolate Peanut Butter Bars, 228, *229*
    Thai-Inspired Steak Salad, *26*27
Pears
    Warm Farro Steak Salad, *32, 33*
Peas
    Chicken Pot Pie Chowder, 54, *55*
    Skillet Chicken and Veggies with "Peanut" Sauce,
        122–23, *123*
Pepper(s). *See also* Chile(s)
    Blackened Sheet Pan Salmon with Jalapeño Tartar
        Sauce, 190, *191*
    Creamy Cajun Fish, 174–75, *175*
    Poblano, Chipotle Turkey–Stuffed, 112, *113*
    Red, Miso Buddha Bowls, 208, *209*
    Roasted Vegetable Pita with Herby Tahini, 202–3,
        *203*
    Sheet Pan Ratatouille with Crispy Gnocchi, *210,*
        211
    Skillet Chicken and Veggies with "Peanut" Sauce,
        122–23, *123*
    Skillet Mojo Pork Tenderloin, 160, *161*
    Sweet Piquanté, and Sausage, Sheet Pan, *142,* 143
Pesto
    Lemon Basil, 8
    Sheet Pan Sausage and Sweet Piquanté Peppers,
        *142,* 143
    Sun-Dried Tomato, and Mint Pasta, *86,* 87
Philly Cheesesteak–Stuffed Mushrooms, *152,* 153
Pickled jalapeños, about, 9
Pineapple
    Jerk-Inspired Chicken Tacos, *124,* 125
Pita, Roasted Vegetable, with Herby Tahini, 202–3,
    *203*
Pork. *See also* Bacon; Sausage(s)
    and Cabbage Stir-Fry, Chili Oil, 154, *155*

Creamy Italian Chopped Salad, *34, 35*
Lemongrass, Lettuce Cups, 148–49, *149*
Tenderloin, Skillet Mojo, 160, *161*
Potato(es). *See also* Sweet Potato(es)
Chicken Pot Pie Chowder, 54, *55*
Leek Soup, Loaded, 62, *63*
Sheet Pan Hot Honey Dijon Chicken, *114,* 115
Sheet Pan Salmon Niçoise, 24–25, *25*
Slow Cooker or Pressure Cooker Spiced Beef
Stew, 68–69, *69*
Poultry. *See* Chicken; Turkey

## Q

Quinoa
Chicken Bake, Skillet BBQ, *110,* 111
Red Pepper Miso Buddha Bowls, 208, *209*

## R

Radishes
Lemongrass Pork Lettuce Cups, 148–49, *149*
Portobello Tacos with Serrano Avocado Crema,
212, *213*
Slow Cooker or Pressure Cooker Gochujang
Shredded Beef Bowls, *138,* 139–40
Raisins
Cady's Carrot Cake, *224,* 225–26
Curried Chicken and Kale Salad with Creamy
Harissa Dressing, *20,* 21
Raspberry Vinaigrette, California Turkey Salad with,
*16,* 17
Ratatouille, Sheet Pan, with Crispy Gnocchi, *210,* 211
Red Snapper Veracruzana, 194, *195*
Rice
Baked Salmon Sushi Bowls with Spicy Mayo, *172,*
173
and Green Chile Chicken Soup, *56,* 57
One-Pan Coconut-Lime Chicken and, 98, *99*
Red Pepper Miso Buddha Bowls, 208, *209*
Saffron-Spiced Shrimp Skillet, *184,* 185
and Sausage Skillet, Cajun, *134, 135*
Slow Cooker or Pressure Cooker Gochujang
Shredded Beef Bowls, *138,* 139–40

## S

Saffron-Spiced Shrimp Skillet, *184,* 185
Salads
BLT Panzanella, *30,* 31

Cajun Cobb, with Shrimp, 36, *37*
California Turkey, with Raspberry Vinaigrette, *16,*
17
Creamy Italian Chopped, *34, 35*
Cucumber-Feta, Mediterranean Salmon Burgers
with, 182, *183*
Curried Chicken and Kale, with Creamy Harissa
Dressing, *20, 21*
Deconstructed Waldorf, *42, 43*
Fattoush, with Creamy Feta Dressing, 28, *29*
Grilled Chicken, with Chili-Lime Dressing, 22,
*23*
Macho, *38, 39*
Sheet Pan Salmon Niçoise, 24–25, *25*
Shredded Kale, with Grapefruit and Seared
Salmon, 14, *15*
Steak, Thai-Inspired, *26*27
Sweet Potato Fry, with Lemon-Tahini Dressing,
40, *41*
Warm Farro Steak, *32, 33*
White Bean and Arugula, Seared Tuna with, 18,
*19*
Salami
Creamy Italian Chopped Salad, *34, 35*
Salmon
Baked, Sushi Bowls with Spicy Mayo, *172,*
173
Blackened Sheet Pan, with Jalapeño Tartar Sauce,
190, *191*
Burgers, Mediterranean, with Cucumber-Feta
Salad, 182, *183*
Crunchy Blackened, Tacos with Serrano Slaw,
176–77, *177*
Niçoise, Sheet Pan, 24–25, *25*
Seared, and Grapefruit, Shredded Kale Salad with,
14, *15*
Salsa verde, about, 9
Sausage(s)
and Butternut Squash Pasta, One-Pot, 72, *73*
Creamy Dijon Penne with Kielbasa, 88, *89*
Easy Italian Wedding Soup, *48,* 49
One-Skillet Lasagna, 80, *81*
and Rice Skillet, Cajun, *134, 135*
and Sweet Piquanté Peppers, Sheet Pan, *142,*
143
and Tomato-Basil Tortellini Soup, 66, *67*
Seafood. *See* Fish; Shrimp

Shrimp
    Cajun Cobb Salad with, *36, 37*
    Lettuce Wraps, Bang Bang, *192,* 193
    and Noodle Soup, Aromatic, 58, *59*
    Roasted, Cherry Tomato, and Feta Pasta, *74,* 75
    Skillet, Saffron-Spiced, *184,* 185
    Stir-Fry, Tom Yum–Inspired, *180,* 181
Sichuan-Inspired Beef Stir-Fry, *166,* 167
Soups
    Black Bean, Simple, 50, *51*
    Chicken Pot Pie Chowder, 54, *55*
    Chicken Tortilla, The Best, 46, *47*
    Green Chile Chicken and Rice, *56,* 57
    Green Curry Chicken, *64,* 65
    Italian Wedding, Easy, *48,* 49
    Lentil, Italian, *60,* 61
    Loaded Potato Leek, 62, *63*
    Shrimp and Noodle, Aromatic, 58, *59*
    Tomato-Basil Tortellini and Sausage, 66, *67*
Sour Cream Chicken Enchiladas, *106,* 107
Spinach
    and Artichokes, Creamy Goat Cheese Pasta with, *82, 83*
    Creamy Cajun Fish, 174–75, *175*
    Curry Chicken Skillet with Sweet Potatoes, 104, *105*
Squash. *See also* Zucchini
    Acorn, Beef Enchilada–Stuffed, 164, *165*
    Butternut, and Sausage Pasta, One-Pot, 72, *73*
    Spaghetti, with Sun-Dried Tomatoes and Mushrooms, *206,* 207
Sriracha, about, 9–11
Stew, Spiced Beef, Slow Cooker or Pressure Cooker, 68–69, *69*
Strawberry
    Oatmeal Bars, 218, *219*
    Short-Crispies, *230,* 231
Sushi Bowls, Baked Salmon, with Spicy Mayo, *172,* 173
Sweet Potato(es)
    Blackened Sheet Pan Salmon with Jalapeño Tartar Sauce, 190, *191*
    and Brussels Sprouts, Sheet Pan Mini BBQ-Cheddar Meatloaves with, *158,* 159
    Curry Chicken Skillet with, 104, *105*
    Fry Salad with Lemon-Tahini Dressing, 40, *41*
    Red Pepper Miso Buddha Bowls, 208, *209*

## T

Tacos
    Beef, Crunchy Baked, 156–57, *157*
    Beer-Braised Chicken, Slow Cooker or Pressure Cooker, 116–17, *117*
    Chicken, Jerk-Inspired, *124,* 125
    Crunchy Blackened Salmon, with Serrano Slaw, 176–77, *177*
    Portobello, with Serrano Avocado Crema, 212, *213*
Tahini
    Herby, Roasted Vegetable Pita with, 202–3, *203*
    -Lemon Dressing, Sweet Potato Fry Salad with, 40, *41*
    Simple Skillet Beef Schwarma, 144, *145*
Tarragon Mushroom Orzo-tto, *94,* 95
Tartar Sauce, Jalapeño, Blackened Sheet Pan Salmon with, 190, *191*
Thai-Inspired Steak Salad, 2627
Tikka Masala-Inspired Lentils, *200,* 201
Tomato(es)
    -Basil Tortellini and Sausage Soup, 66, *67*
    The Best Chicken Tortilla Soup, 46, *47*
    BLT Panzanella, *30, 31*
    Bursting, Italian Skirt Steak with, 136, *137*
    Cajun Cobb Salad with Shrimp, *36, 37*
    Calabrian Chile Pasta Pomodoro, 92, *93*
    Cherry, Roasted Shrimp, and Feta Pasta, *74,* 75
    Chipotle Turkey–Stuffed Poblano Peppers, 112, *113*
    Creamy Italian Chopped Salad, *34, 35*
    Curried Chili, *52, 53*
    Fattoush Salad with Creamy Feta Dressing, 28, *29*
    Greek-Inspired Chicken and Orzo Bake, *128,* 129
    Grilled Chicken Salad with Chili-Lime Dressing, *22, 23*
    Herby Mediterranean Baked Meatballs, *146,* 147
    Jalapeño Tuna Cake Melts, *188,* 189
    Macho Salad, *38, 39*
    Red Snapper Veracruzana, 194, *195*
    Roasted Fish and White Bean Puttanesca, 170, *171*
    Sheet Pan Ratatouille with Crispy Gnocchi, *210,* 211
    Skillet Chicken Cacciatore, *100,* 101
    sun-dried, 11

Sun-Dried, and Mushrooms, Spaghetti Squash with, *206, 207*
Sun-Dried, Pesto, and Mint Pasta, *86,* 87
Tom Yum–Inspired Shrimp Stir-Fry, *180,* 181
Tom Yum–Inspired Shrimp Stir-Fry, *180,* 181
Tortilla chips
    The Best Chicken Tortilla Soup, 46, *47*
    Grilled Chicken Salad with Chili-Lime Dressing, *22, 23*
Tortillas
    Chipotle Cauliflower Tostadas, 198, *199*
    Crunchy Baked Beef Tacos, 156–57, *157*
    Crunchy Blackened Salmon Tacos with Serrano Slaw, 176–77, *177*
    Jerk-Inspired Chicken Tacos, *124,* 125
    Portobello Tacos with Serrano Avocado Crema, 212, *213*
    Sour Cream Chicken Enchiladas, *106,* 107
Tostadas, Chipotle Cauliflower, 198, *199*
Tuna
    Cake Melts, Jalapeño, *188,* 189
    Seared, with White Bean and Arugula Salad, 18, *19*
Turkey
    Chipotle, –Stuffed Poblano Peppers, 112, *113*
    Ground, Stir-Fry, Ginger and Peanut Butter, 130, *131*
    Salad, California, with Raspberry Vinaigrette, *16,* 17
2 a.m. Kimchi Noodles, 76, 77

**V**

Vegetables. *See specific vegetables*

**W**

Waldorf Salad, Deconstructed, *42,* 43
Walnuts
    Deconstructed Waldorf Salad, *42,* 43
    Warm Farro Steak Salad, *32, 33*
White chocolate
    Strawberry Short-Crispies, *230, 231*

**Y**

Yogurt
    Blackened Sheet Pan Salmon with Jalapeño Tartar Sauce, 190, *191*
    Deconstructed Waldorf Salad, *42,* 43
    Greek, about, 6
    Herby Mediterranean Baked Meatballs, *146,* 147
    Jerk-Inspired Chicken Tacos, *124,* 125

**Z**

Za'atar-Crusted Lamb Chops with Roasted Carrots and Herb Drizzle, 150, *151*
Zucchini
    Roasted Vegetable Pita with Herby Tahini, 202–3, *203*
    Sheet Pan Ratatouille with Crispy Gnocchi, *210,* 211
    Sun-Dried Tomato, Pesto, and Mint Pasta, *86,* 87

HarperCollins books may be purchased for educational,
business, or sales promotional use. For information,
please email the Special Markets Department at
SPsales@harpercollins.com.

FIRST EDITION

DESIGNED BY RENATA DE OLIVEIRA

*Photography by Kristen Kilpatrick*

Library of Congress Cataloging-in-Publication Data

Names: Snodgrass, Alex, author. | Kilpatrick, Kristen,
photographer.

Title: Dinner tonight : 100 simple, healthy recipes for
every night of the week / Alex Snodgrass ; photography
by Kristen Kilpatrick.

Description: First edition. | New York, NY : William
Morrow, [2023]. | Includes index. | Summary: "New York
Times bestselling author and queen of healthy weeknight
dinners Alex Snodgrass shares delicious dinners that will
bring everyone to the table"— Provided by publisher.

Identifiers: LCCN 2023013425 | ISBN 9780063278479
(hardcover) | ISBN 9780063278486 (ebook)

Subjects: LCSH: Dinners and dining. | Quick and easy
cooking.

Classification: LCC TX737 .S6473 2023 | DDC 641.5/4—
dc23/eng/20230331

LC record available at https://lccn.loc.gov/2023013425

ISBN 978-0-06-327847-9

24 25 26  TC  10 9 8 7 6 5 4 3 2